A Guide to Managing and Leading School Operations

A Guide to Managing and Leading School Operations

The Principal's Field Manual

Jerome Cranston

ROWMAN & LITTLEFIELD
Lanham • Boulder • New York • London

Published by Rowman & Littlefield
A wholly owned subsidiary of
The Rowman & Littlefield Publishing Group, Inc.
4501 Forbes Boulevard, Suite 200, Lanham, Maryland 20706
https://rowman.com

Unit A, Whitacre Mews, 26-34 Stannary Street, London SE11 4AB,
United Kingdom

British Library Cataloguing in Publication Information Available

Library of Congress Cataloging-in-Publication Data

Names: Cranston, Jerome, author.
Title: A guide to managing and leading school operations : the principal's
    field manual / Jerome Cranston.
Description: Lanham : Rowman & Littlefield, a wholly owned subsidiary of The
    Rowman & Littlefield Publishing Group, Inc., [2018] | Includes
    bibliographical references and index.
Identifiers: LCCN 2017053643 (print) | LCCN 2018001868 (ebook) | ISBN
    9781475839791 (Electronic) | ISBN 9781475839777 (cloth : alk. paper) |
    ISBN 9781475839784 (pbk. : alk. paper)
Subjects: LCSH: Public schools--Business management--Handbooks, manuals, etc.
Classification: LCC LB2823.5 (ebook) | LCC LB2823.5 .C7 2018 (print) | DDC
    371.2/06--dc23
LC record available at https://lccn.loc.gov/2017053643

∞ ™ The paper used in this publication meets the minimum requirements of American
National Standard for Information Sciences Permanence of Paper for Printed Library
Materials, ANSI/NISO Z39.48-1992.

Printed in the United States of America

Dedication

It is a regrettable truth but one I have come to recognize over time. I have foolishly tried to live a life for two. Not because you would have expected me to do so. I know that is not true. You rarely expected anything more from me than to be your brother. No, I did so rather because it is all I could offer in an attempt to honor you. I have no doubt in my mind that I have not succeeded in such an impossible and somewhat emotionally immature aspiration. I have accepted the contentment that comes with admitting such a failing to myself and carrying on with life. It is, after all, all that we can do: carry on living as best as we are able and in doing so hope that we bring honor to those who have shaped us.

Contents

Foreword

What a pleasure it is to write a foreword for a book that "keeps it real" for all of us who know what it is like to be in the "middle of the muddle" of educational administration. The book you are about to enjoy acknowledges the role of visionary leadership while also recognizing the importance of daily management practice in what are arguably three of the most important functions of school administration: personnel, finance, and risk management. Though the content of this book is targeted to in-school administrative teams (principals in particular), it will also be of interest to senior administrators, school boards, teachers, and parents who desire to work with forward-thinking principals who are competent and confident in the daily management of schools. Principals who conduct their management practice according to the principles outlined in this text will find that they inspire confidence in the people most affected by their decisions. These principals create the conditions in which the primary aims of schools—teaching and learning—are facilitated.

The content of this book is organized into sections that offer principles and practices for principals to consider as ways of thinking about and acting on administrative tasks. Each chapter is framed by a quotation that speaks to the responsibility principals have as political actors in whom the public trust has been placed. Dr. Cranston draws from a number of literary, historic, philosophic, and scholarly sources to provide support for his ideas that irreverently question the empty rhetoric of leadership literature that "baffles with bullshit" without providing concrete direction for those who have been granted the opportunity to lead schools.

The ideas presented in this text are grounded in practice and experience. Dr. Cranston articulates well that, although schools are becoming more complex spaces, the primary functions of school administration remain quite consistent. Although he remains optimistic that school leaders can, and do, lead and manage well, he also acknowledges the failing of the education system to put in place school leaders who are thoughtful, accountable, and ethical. Cranston suggests that, although no foolproof answers for leadership exist for school principals, it is the responsibility of each principal to make decisions that are grounded in current realities, thoughtfully researched to support long-term and short-term ends, and accountable to those who are affected by them. He provides concrete suggestions on how to achieve these ends and advocates that principals should make no apologies for holding true to principles that build trust, provide a sense of direction for the school, and affirm those who are working hard to improve the educative process for all.

In a clear and concise manner, Dr. Cranston helps the reader think about what is truly important in school leadership and the manner in which school leaders can move toward those aims. He challenges the tendency for school leaders to act in ways that are "good enough" and reminds us of the steward-ship necessary by those responsible for maintaining public confidence and trust in the education system. His work cuts through the mysticism inherent in current "pop culture" leadership circles, and he rightly challenges the notion that "anyone can lead." In his view, character, competence, and hard work matter.

As someone who has had the pleasure of being an administrative col-league of Jerome's, I can attest that he is someone who "walks his talk." Jerome provides a type of leadership that is grounded in principles of prac-tice, and he takes his role as steward of the public trust seriously. As a faculty member in the field of educational administration and a current administra-tor, I am someone who regularly who thinks about, acts on, and teaches about educational administration. The examples of the text resonate with me. When I read them, I can picture the faces of people I have hired and fired. I can recall making financial decisions that were the impetus of some programs and the death knell to others. I can recall crisis events that were handled well and others that had horrible consequences for those whose lives were af-fected. I have to live with the consequences of all of those decisions, good or bad, on myself and on all of those I impacted because of my role as an administrator. There is a huge responsibility in that, and some of those les-sons were hard to learn. In the end, as Jerome articulates, the "proof is in the pudding" when it comes to school administration. Principals who have the inspirational talent to put together the right ingredients at the right time matter to all of us, today and in the future.

Dr. Dawn Wallin
Professor and Associate Dean
Undergraduate Programs, Partnerships and Research
College of Education

University of Saskatchewan
Saskatchewan, Canada

Defining Terms

PRINCIPLE   noun   A fundamental truth or proposition that serves as the foundation for a system of belief or behaviour or for a chain of reasoning: example – *the basic principles of teaching.*

PRACTICE   noun   The actual application or use of an idea, belief or method, as opposed to the theories relating to it: example – *the practices of teaching.*

BREATHING SPACE   noun   An opportunity to pause, relax or decide what to do next: example – *school administrators relish the infrequent breathing spaces that serendipitously appear in the busyness of the school day.*

Preface

Chi Wan thought three times before taking action. When the Master was informed of it, he said, "Twice will do."
—Confucius, a Chinese teacher, editor, politician, and philosopher in the fourth and fifth centuries BC

Confucius offered sobering advice to leaders: Think hard before acting; however, then be decisive when acting. In the era of whimsical advice from purveyors of leadership lore, those who want to be leaders ought to (a) leap without assessing the consequences and concern for the results of their actions or (b) not act at all and instead rely on the status quo to see them through. Confucius insisted that thinking and rethinking before acting was wise. In simple terms, it makes sense to look before you leap. Many of us learned that lesson the hard way. But as school leaders it is important to not look for so long that you succumb to "paralysis by analysis."

This book is a collection of ideas about the business operations of schools. It represents an expression of the sense I made from over two decades of experience as a school leader myself, first as a principal and then as a superintendent of schools, and also from working with cohort after cohort of future school leaders as a professor of educational administration and leadership. It provides perspectives—developed by me, the author—that do not purport to have greater exactitude than some of the perspectives you hold. The facts contained in the book might be seen as simply a representation of what English philosopher and mathematician Alfred North Whitehead once referred to as "inert knowledge." They are, indeed, just truthful propositions that only gain meaning by being placed in a context that makes sense to you, the reader. However, it is hoped that the knowledge shared here will not remain inert for very long, but instead be utilized, tested, and put into new combinations as you begin to consider how the issues raised here affect not only the generalized business of schools but also your particular school's business affairs.

PRINCIPLES, PRACTICES, AND BREATHING SPACES

It is greatly important that, when I write about the principles and practices of school leadership and management for "principals" throughout this book, you recognize it is not my suggestion that vice and associate principals should be excluded from the claims I am stating. I know firsthand that vice and associate principals are very involved in leading and managing a school's business operations and ought to be.

Simply for ease of writing I have conveniently used the term "principals" to identify principals, vice and associate principals, as well as other permutations of the sanctioned leadership team in a school, without having to write out the title for each administrative position. Thus, please understand that I am not proposing that both the principles and also practices of effectively managing the business operations of schools are exclusively the realm of the school principal. I am not interested in promoting dictatorial leadership or conversely fascist management.

That said, educational leaders are always looking for simple ways to apply good principles (patterns of advice) with meaningful practices (specific actions). It makes quite a bit of sense that school leaders would look to align these two things: principles, or value-based ideas that provide them with a conceptual framework they can understand, and practices, the actionable manifestations of those principles.

In simple terms, the difference between principles and practices can be illustrated as follows:

- **Principle 1.0:** *Be prepared.*
- **Practice 1.0:** *Buy a plunger before you need a plunger.*

The maxim "Be prepared" is a timeless principle that some may recognize as the motto of the Boy and Girl Scouts from the early 1900s, but it is obviously a principle that has existed for well over a century. This principle is, however, one that is worth remembering to avoid the messiness that presents itself in so many facets of life. "Buy a plunger before you need a plunger" is a practice that should be enacted by every homeowner and/or renter and anyone who claims to be a leader. It is connected to the principle of being prepared and, when enacted, can help avoid the inevitability of having to stand ankle deep in the muck while waiting for a plumber—someone who can manage matters—to arrive and deal with the mess. Practices like the one illustrated here are, in fact, applications of a principle in a specific context, and sometimes they can be etched into consciousness in some very memorable ways. In short, principles are good ideas and/or represent valued ideals that are stated in a context-independent manner. Practices are applications of these principles stated in very context-dependent ways.

Outside of the principles and practices paradigm is a third sort of space that this book will intentionally cultivate. Administrative life is not all principles and practices. Administrative life is in reality punctuated by occasional breathing spaces that show up in the form of a respite, a reflective moment, a relational interaction, or, at times, a small revelation. In practical terms, these breathing spaces are critically important moments in time that happen between moments of leadership and management. These serendipitous pauses are usually unplanned and irregularly materialize in the midst of being enthralled with the excitement of "big picture" or "out of the box" leadership thinking and the daily routine of managing the operations of the school. The breathing spaces that punctuate moments in the book are a sort of storied reflection that synthesizes and draws on my own experiences with the business side of school administration. They offer anecdotes meant to help us consider what really happens when leadership and management converge.

This book is therefore focused on the principles and practices of effectively leading and managing the business operations of schools but is also anchored in the unpredictability that characterizes the principalship. Use this book as a guide and a frame of reference, but do not mistake its contents as the absolute authority on the subject of leading and managing schools.

Leading and managing schools needs to be a deliberative and thoughtful act. Leading and managing such complex social institutions as schools requires activating the right skills and knowledge at the right time. There is no room for merely inert knowledge when a future or current staff member, student, or other stakeholder is seeking solutions and support. Being responsible for the well-being of others requires those who lead and manage to take action. So yes, it is certainly about how one should act.

Leading and managing schools also requires a modicum of faith, a faith that both leadership vision and management prowess can be enacted by a principal who is committed to each. This book attempts to illuminate some aspects of that act of faith to make them slightly less opaque. And in the end, I hope it offers an encouraging perspective that enacting both leading and managing and carving out the right amount of breathing space for reflection are not only possible but also can be accomplished exceptionally well.

Acknowledgments

I wish to sincerely thank the following people and organizations for their encouragement and intellectual and emotional support that allowed me to create this book: Janet Cranston, my best friend, life partner, and ever-willing reader, who always offers a caring yet soberly honest appraisal of my far-fetched ideas; Kristin Kusanovich, my writing and research collaborative partner from Santa Clara University, for her thoughtful suggestions about how to keep the artistry alive in the tone and tenor of the words and how to structure the paragraphs to fashion the sights and sounds that exist in my mind; Joanne Struch, Stephanie Crook, and Emily Janssens for their willingness to read and suggest revisions to various iterations of this book; Sherry Bestvater and Rachel Thiessen, a pair of former graduate students who ooze common sense and know-how and work tirelessly as educators, chasing after approaches to increase students' chances of finding success and who ensured that the lofty ideas contained in the book's pages mostly touched the ground that the committed, hardworking school leaders tread on; and, finally, to my home faculty of education at the University of Manitoba for tolerating my need for time and space to continue to act scholarly.

Chapter One

Introduction to Leading and Managing the Business of Schools

Day by day, what you choose, what you think and what you do is who you become.
—Heraclitus of Ephesus, a pre-Socratic Greek philosopher in the fourth and fifth centuries BC

The false dichotomy that separates "leadership" from "management" has led far too many to ignore the reality that every day we make choices—some big, some small—and how we act through those choices contributes greatly to how we are regarded. In simple terms, how school leaders manage the business operations of the school—how they act—says a whole lot more than the leadership "bon mots" they hand out at staff meetings that are intended to either inspire or mollify their followers.

When I first became a school principal, I was ecstatic. Finally, I thought, after three years of teaching and following someone else's vision of teaching and learning, I was being given the opportunity to lead a school. In the euphoria of being named the leader, I did my very best to ignore the fact that I really did not have a clue what a school principal did in terms of managing the school's operations or leading the people invested in the school for that matter. I had a fairly thorough understanding of how to lead learners in a classroom and the importance of coalescing parental support, but I did not have any of the business skills required of the principalship. In the back of my mind I was willing to accept that comforting euphemism that "it does not matter that I didn't know what I didn't know," and by imagining this to be true, I was able to allow any momentary lapses of feeling inadequate to fade. When encountering unknowns, I kept thinking these three things:

1. How hard could it really be?
2. What I didn't know I could learn from a book.
3. That book would be a sort of easy-to-follow instruction manual for the aspiring principal.

"Certainly," I told myself, "someone has written the award-winning *School Administration for Dummies in Seven Illustrated Steps*, specifically for people like me."

During the eight years that I spent as a principal and the five I subsequently served as a superintendent, I never found such a book. I also learned that there are very few dummies who get to be school leaders.

THE VALUE OF PRACTICAL WISDOM

Over the past years, I have had the privilege of lecturing about various aspects of school leadership—on such topics as personnel management, school finance, and educational law—and I have become somewhat perplexed by the fact that there is very little written that integrates those three topics with practical wisdom. Though it is not true that you can learn everything from a book, books can indeed launch an important process of learning. It seemed like this integration of principles and practices of the business operations of schools was a gap that I might be able to help fill because the "build your wings while falling out of the skies" model of learning how to lead was, to put it mildly, a painfully stressful prospect.

The principalship is tough work that exacts a psychosocial and emotional toll on those who are willing to take on the responsibilities. Anyone who lives in a state of denial that the responsibilities that come with being the school's principal, as rewarding as they might be, are not stressful is simply deluding him- or herself. I also learned that the problem with the third point referred to earlier is that while it sounds catchy as an advertising phrase for the "do it yourself" outfits trying to lure customers away from the temptation of using professionally sourced advice, it is not in actuality a sound plan for a school principal. No matter how adept an individual is at learning, the ignorance associated with being a new principal is anything but blissful, and DIY approaches to school administration may lead to dreadful results that put students, teachers, and entire school communities at a level of risk they should never have to stomach.

It seems futile to debate whether or not contemporary school environments have become more complex and diverse over the past few decades. The truth is that we live and teach in an era in which all children are expected to learn and in which high learning standards set a vision of what educational success means, practically speaking, for all students. In a rapidly changing and more technologically oriented society, students will need to acquire the knowledge and skills that will help them achieve success not only in school but also in life once formalized learning is complete. The evolving nature of school environments has placed new demands on educational leaders.

Prior to embarking on my first principalship, I was already pursing a graduate degree specializing in educational administration with a focus on teacher professional development. I was content with the thought that this program of studies would help prepare me to take on the role of instructional leader, and to a degree it did. It certainly helped my own growth and development as an administrator to come to a better understanding of how teachers professionally grow and develop throughout their careers and to learn what forms of support might work at certain stages of their development.

What came as a surprise quite early in my tenure as a school administrator, though, was that instead of developing teachers professionally all day long, a fair amount of my time and energy would be spent dealing with personnel issues, reconciling poorly conceived and constructed school budgets, and trying my best to avoid some of the legal pitfalls that some days seemed to arrive with overwhelming urgency. From the moment I was hired and assumed a formal school leadership role, I was confronted with the complex challenge of recruiting and retaining a cadre of qualified teachers while maintaining a balanced budget to ensure that each and every child in the school received his or her legal due, which was an education that was appropriately tailored to his or her needs without exposing him or her to undue risk. It was no easy feat to accomplish, and not one that I always gracefully accomplished. It was, in reality, a role for which my graduate studies had done little to prepare me.

Today there is a premium placed on developing principals, vice principals, and all upper-level school staff as educational leaders who are also great instructional leaders. And that is not such a bad thing. While gaining knowledge of and developing skills in personnel management, finance, legal compliance, and government mandates were once the primary areas of focus in the preparation of school leaders, over the past thirty years newer educational initiatives have emphasized the development of instructional leadership skills to promote good teaching and high levels of student achievement. Arguably, now more than ever before, educational leaders are being urged to recognize and assume a shared responsibility not only for students' intellectual and educational development but also for students' and staff's personal, social, emotional, and physical development. The increasing diversity of school communities places a premium on school leaders who can create a vision of success for all students and use their skills in communication, collaboration, and community building to ensure the vision becomes a reality.

It is widely accepted these days that highly effective principals have the ability to enhance the academic success of a typical student in their schools through indirect influence on the teaching and learning dynamic, while ineffective principals conversely lower student achievement. And while differences in teacher quality will also have a direct impact on students, only the students in their particular classroom will presumably be affected. On the other hand, differences in principal effectiveness are felt by everyone and affect all students in a given school. It is easy to see why. Today the spotlight shines on school accountability and student learning in most school leadership preparation programs and textbooks, and professional development sessions are focused on developing leadership capacity without much attention given to what it means to manage a school's operations. After all, management tasks do not seem to immediately raise test scores, nor do they seem to directly build the instructional capacity of the staff. Lastly, they are just unglamorous sounding.

The problem is that it is dangerous to separate school "leadership" from "management" and then make broad generalizations about the differences of importance between "managing" and "leading" schools. Most of the literature these days suggests that one (leadership) should be more prized than the other (management).

Right now, school leadership is an "in vogue" phrase, while school management is often used to malign the administrative functions that few in formal leadership positions actually enjoy doing. An often-quoted phrase by keynote presenters at school leadership conferences is: Managers do things right, while leaders do the right thing. What they may not realize, though, is that such divinatory tidings are a paraphrase of the words of Warren G. Bennis and Burt Nanus, two of the so-called gurus of the management literature, who contend that leadership and management are diametrically opposed concepts and practices. I encountered the work of Bennis and Nanus early on in my graduate studies in educational administration, sometime in the mid-1990s, and soon learned that these two respected authorities on leadership were adamant that no one individual could be both a leader and a manager. Leaders and managers have, in their estimation, fundamentally different values and personalities. Such a distinction clearly cast the manager as the dependable plodder, while the leader was the sophisticated executive, scanning the horizon and strategizing. It is hard to argue with the fact that they have sold tens of thousands of copies on their books.

This bias against management tasks and management identity seems to only attract more book buyers and attendees to professional leadership development institutes. After all, most people would rather be and be seen as a sophisticated executive than a dependable plodder. The "lead not manage" exhortation is alluring. If nothing more, imagine the difference in footwear between the "plodder" and the "sophisticant."

At its worst, however, specific abuses of the term "management" are intended to pejoratively place some people in the "Dunce's Corner." All too often, teachers and principals will proclaim such virtuous statements as "Schools should not be run by bean counters" or "What do those cold-hearted human-resource-types know about teaching?" Or, when faced with an issue that requires legal expertise, they will petulantly offer that it is time to "send in the lawyers," a sarcastic play on the title of the 1973 Stephen Sondheim song "Send in the Clowns" from the musical *A Little Night Music*. Those witty educators most likely know they lack specific expertise that pertains directly to the legal issues at hand. But instead of wondering about that gap in their preparation, they both need and dismiss the "clowns" simultaneously, implying that those wretched so-called managers better do their job but better not compare themselves to leaders of schools.

It should be no wonder, then, that management is too often dismissed as a soulless and number-crunching exercise in hounding people about the minutiae and making them fill out forms, while leadership is lionized as "big picture thinking" and "inspiring the troops." As a result, people aspire to be leaders while blindly accepting that managing well is not that important, and besides, they conclude, managing is mind numbing. Except that to falsely separate leadership, which sells well under the marketing banner of "creativity" these days, and make management sound like dull drudgery is to set up the next generation of school administrators for something unattainable, that is, effective leadership without the requisite school management acumen.

The leadership and management of schools play equally important functions in executing and integrating school improvement initiatives. Management is about stewardship. Effectively managing the business operations of a school means offering predictability, reliability, and, to as much of a degree as is possible, certainty to the organizational processes and outcomes. Effective managers attempt to forecast the effects of the change process by gathering information about the present and past state of the school's operations to help steer it clear of hazards and navigate during turbulent times. In every industry and business, even in such a people-intensive operation as a school, change ebbs and flows in repeated cycles so that at least to some extent, change can be charted and therefore anticipated. Such awareness allows, in some cases, for change to be merely endured, while at other times change can be used as a springboard to flourish.

True enough, schools are disruptive, messy, and complicated organizations. Even with the best-laid plans, events rarely occur exactly as they were predicted. However, almost everything in a school's operational infrastructure, namely personnel employed, financial commitments, and business continuity plans, mutually influence the other aspects of the school's operations. It is consequently the responsibility of those who administer schools to understand the organizational operations of schools so that ideas and innovations intended to improve the educational opportunities for students can become tangible rather than simply remain as abstract notions, or worse, become dicey risks that can lead to bankruptcy, something no clowns can fix.

Leadership, on the other hand, when separated from management seems to be less about taking care of things that are really present and more about creating something that does not already exist and convincing people to commit to the work of moving toward it. Leadership that stands alone from so-called management is concerned with breakthrough, innovation, and discovery, all of which require a disruption of the status quo. Leadership challenges the existing mindsets of people. Change can, of course, be good or bad.

The irony of the dismissed but desperately needed manager is matched by the view of leadership that is so easily revered but that is capable of creating absurdly complicated and unnecessary work. To return to the example of preparedness and the concrete image of the plunger, management would not use a plunger if the pipes weren't backed up but would instead turn its attention to another real need, while leadership might throw the plunger out the window and convene a team to design an object that unclogs a toilet. While management has been cast as operating by the maxim "if it is not broken, do not fix it," leadership professes "if it is not broken, break it and build it anew." However, this binary hides the truth of what it means to be an educational leader. To be an engaged school leader means that one must be both visionary and reflective while staying in the fray of the daily operations of the school—the hectic, fragmented, never-ending world of managing the school's business operations. It is purported that Stanford University professor emeritus James G. March maintained that leadership involves plumbing as well as poetry. I would agree that the convergence of applying the two concepts provides a formidable resource for school administrators to draw on.

CONVERGENCE OF LEADERSHIP AND MANAGEMENT

Management, argues Henry Mintzberg (an internationally recognized professor of management studies and respected author on business and management), is more art than science, more based on insight, vision, and intuition—yes, he does mean intuition. What Mintzberg is suggesting is that management is not an endeavor cemented in place by the rote memorization of procedural handbooks or the obsession with following mind-numbing rules, as is all too often operationalized by technocrats.

Perhaps what has been missing in the conversation about leading and managing schools is a more integrative understanding of the two concepts and one that provides a distinction between leading and managing the business operations of schools while also clearly recognizing the expectation that it is the responsibility of school leaders to enact both. Irrespective of how the terms are defined, school leaders will experience difficulty in deciding the balance between higher-order tasks designed to improve staff, student, and school performance (leadership) and routine maintenance of organizational operations (management) if they have not considered how the two functions—leading and managing—might complement each other. Figure 1.1 is meant to provide a simplistic visual representation of the complex space that exists where the two concepts converge.

The reality is that both leadership and management serve vital roles in all organizational systems, and schools are no exceptions to this fact. It is unfortunate that these days it is far more glamorous to be a leader than it is to be a manager. Such folly comes with a price to pay, says Mintzberg, who maintains that, while leadership and management are very different responsibilities, neither is achievable without the other. Mintzberg laments that most leadership preparation programs offered these days treat management as the ugly stepsister, and far too many organizations are overled and undermanaged.

Without grounding in the knowledge and skills to ensure that an innovative initiative to improve teaching and learning schoolwide can access the necessary financial and human resources and will comply with the pertinent statutes and regulations, none of the leader's grand ideas are worth much of anything. Future possibilities need to be situated in present-day realities. This

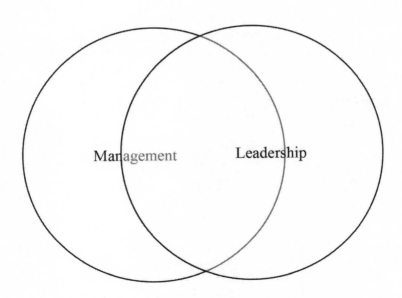

Figure 1.1.   Management and Leadership Convergence

is not to suggest that visionary ideas and conversations must be cemented into simply conserving the status quo of schooling. What is needed are school leaders who can bridge the seeming dichotomy between being the steward of the public's trust and having a vision for a future.

More than ever before it seems that we need educational leaders who can honor continuity and stability on one hand, yet are working toward developing new possibilities on the other. It requires synthesist thinking and the ability to entertain what many people regard as opposing perspectives, with both perspectives having validity and informing what needs to be done. Howard Gardener, the John H. and Elisabeth A. Hobbs Professor of Cognition and Education at the Harvard Graduate School of Education, explains that the synthesizing mind takes information from disparate sources, understands and evaluates that information, and puts it together in ways that are meaningful not only to the synthesizer but also to others. It is not enough for a leader to understand her or his thoughts alone. It is imperative that those who are asked to follow are invited to have a clear understanding of the aspirations—as in priorities—that will move the school operations forward.

In close to twenty-five years of work in educational administration from the kindergarten to grade 12 system right through to the postsecondary education system, I have discovered that, as I honed my management skills (specifically in matters related to personnel and financial leadership and legal compliance), I became a more "followable" leader. Staffs were more willing to give me the "benefit of doubt," even when I was not quite sure I knew where I was taking us because they believed I had the skills to navigate the course we were collectively setting. I did not possess some leadership charm that hypnotized the masses into following me. I simply and dutifully cared about the well-being of the people in the organization, especially the ones with the least amount of professional leverage, worked hard to stay within the parameters of the budget by never asking for more when I could find savings within, and did my best to avoid placing anyone or the organization into unfair risky scenarios in which there was far more to lose than there was to gain.

I have observed that school leaders who have the combination of knowledge, skills, and attributes to both manage and lead can have a tremendously positive effect on schools. They can relieve a staff of the doubt that befalls any group when it feels it is being "mismanaged" and more easily allow staff to simply commit to the hard work of teaching and learning. The combination of possessing the knowledge and skills to be considered both a good manager and good leader is rare and valuable and is far more useful than either one alone. Learning to lead means committing oneself to an ongoing journey of being attentive to the organizational reality, both past and present, and generating new possibilities that will offer greater educational opportunities that lead to success for all students. Furthermore, a great leader/manager has to be able to articulate all of these ideas in plain language, not just the managerial ones and not just the visionary ones but all.

This book considers that successful schools need effective administrators skilled and knowledgeable in leadership and management and tries to explain how these mutually influence each other. It is time to stop debating about which one is better, sexier, or more needed in today's schools. It is time to better prepare those responsible for administrative roles to do both. In this knowledge-creation era, developing the capacity of school leaders who are strategic visionaries while at precisely the same time are astute operational implementers seems vital.

COMPLEXITY WITHOUT GRATUITOUS COMPLICATION

I have a confession to make: I do not use Facebook, but I follow the kinds of speech patterns that arise in this popular social media platform. It seems like a lot of work to maintain an account only to have some person I knew in grade 7, who has nothing better to do but "creep" around the Internet, find me, reach out, and so-called friend me. I prefer Twitter. In response to the disclosure that I am not on Facebook but am on Twitter, a professional colleague who barely knew me commented, "Twitter is so cold, so clinical, so heartless. It's not nearly as friendly, warm, and inviting as Facebook." To which I replied, "Exactly. Warmth from adult strangers I happened to have sat next to at a mandatory workshop on interpersonal sensitivity training in middle school social studies class is not the kind of cordiality I seek. I'll take the heartless tweet instead."

I have, however, learned a few things about Facebook from listening to folks, such as how the meaning of the phrase "it's complicated" is an acceptable form of ending a conversation; whether it intends to obscure or deflect truth I am not sure. Though I have heard all about that ambiguous relationship status post, I have yet to hear from anyone what that status really means, at least in practical terms.

In a similar fashion, I have listened to the banter over cheap hors d'oeuvres at academic receptions about the themes presented about managing and leading schools and been left with the impression that when pointy-headed professors or finely tailored keynote presenters want to leave you with a sense that any potential innovation to the business operations of a school must be so enigmatic that it is impossible to "solve," they, too, give the relationship status post to their own relationship with their job. Often they offer that it is, well, complicated, as in too complicated to explain, ascertain, tease out, and even analyze clearly.

This translates into frustration for principals who are looking for practical suggestions about how to improve their schools. And, admittedly, while some published academic keynote-giving cocktail partygoers may want you to believe that "it's complicated" translates into "I can understand it from my vantage point but will never be able to communicate that to an inquiring principal" or even "wouldn't you like to know," I would suggest you slowly walk away either thinking to yourself or perhaps inaudibly mumbling "no."

To be truthful, I am not sure that the use of the phrase "it's complicated" denotes anything either useful or accurate with respect to school operations. Is it really complicated? Or rather, are schools just an example of a complex social system that requires a disciplined focus to understand how best to both lead and manage? Schools are inherently complex. This much is true. They are prime examples of the types of social institutions that operate as if they were complex living ecosystems. Schools are, indeed, systems that do not work terribly well when attempts are made to control them and set them on narrowly defined and tightly constrained linear paths intended to solve clearly identified problems. Yes, it is difficult to lead and manage a school's business operations, but it is dangerous to think it is impossible or so complicated that we can't roll up our sleeves and get to work.

One issue with leading complex social institutions like schools is that complexity is ambiguous and confusing and tends to generate stress. Stress in turn induces fear—fear of change. As a result, in an attempt to reduce the ambiguity inherent in schools, they have been organized into smaller, more easily managed parts. We call these manageable parts such things as elementary, junior high, or senior high schools, or sometimes we configure groups of people under the banner of grade levels, subject area departments, or focus areas. The truth is that fragmentation is a common strategy people use to try to control and manage complexity, and, in part, it is used to try to avoid the commonly felt negative emotions that accompany stressful situations that come with nebulous mobs of people who may have competing interests. We try to master complex problems by compartmentalizing them into specific parts. We attempt, often futilely, to solve a problem by focusing on a few key parts in isolation from the others. We persistently approach personnel challenges, for example, in isolation from the financial implications or legal ramifications that accompany any decision made even though we know the parts are connected and interrelated and that any potential solution is never really that effective when it is developed in isolation.

Similarly, one way to avoid the complexity of managing is to take flight from it. Some leaders simply exist in a lofty arena of vision and "blue sky" dreaming as a way of not having to be grounded whatsoever. The so-called educational leaders get some other person to do things for a school—someone who has been designated as the "administrator" to manage things—and then attribute all of the success that ensues from the efforts of these hardworking managers to their own leadership vision and declare that it is "clearly working." These leaders are not only leaning way too hard on their more competent colleagues and taking credit for other people's work, but they have also forgotten to keep one foot on the ground while their eyes focus on what exists in the heavens above.

LEADING WITH A FOOT ON THE GROUND

I have tried and will continue to make the argument that leading and managing schools are inseparable concepts in a truly effective administrative practice and are what is called for in all schools. I will also, at the outset, propose that it is easier to profess this and have readers agree than it is to put the concepts into practice. But both can be achieved.

By way of example, it is possible to illustrate the two functions—leading and managing—in a matrix that demonstrates how they can exist together and interact yet stymy attempts to improve the educational opportunities of students (see figure 1.2).

Weak Leader/Weak Manager

It seems sensible to start with what everyone obviously strives to avoid. The first priority is to not hand the principalship over to an ineffective administrator who neither plans well nor has the insight to establish important future-oriented goals. This individual is not only ineffective at managing the business operations of the school or system but is also equally ineffectual at leading people. No one chooses to follow these types of managers because they are in way over their heads. Sometimes, however, you find yourself stuck having to listen to them because someone mistakenly made them the boss. Fortunately, as is most often the case, the weak leader/weak manager does not usually last long in a position of power or influence. Unfortunately, though, in a short period of time this individual does leave a legacy of problems for whoever steps into the administrative role immediately after.

	Management	
Leadership	Strong Leader/Weak Manager	Strong Leader/Strong Manager
	Weak Leader/Weak Manager	Weak Leader/Strong Manager

Figure 1.2.   Leading and Managing Matrix

Weak Leader/Strong Manager

This administrator is adept at preparing excellent plans, reconciling budgets, and hiring staff based on the sole criteria of needing to fill vacant positions with simply "good enough" hires. These administrators are often the ones who write annual school plans year after year that are focused on staying the course. They offer no new initiatives or ideas that might propel the teaching and learning dynamic into uncharted territory by challenging the current state of affairs in the school. The weak leader/strong manager is focused on conserving the status quo of what seemingly works even when it does not. Their motto is "this too shall pass," which might be a decent mantra to repeat if you are thinking about kidney stones. But I have been told even passing those little suckers is excruciatingly painful.

Strong Leader/Weak Manager

These administrators are likely to take their school or district right over a cliff as they run out of resources (financial and/or human), break laws, or attempt the clearly impossible. These are the visionaries who want "blue sky" ideas and try them out without regard for the costs associated with the initiative or what is and is not permissible by law. The strong leader/weak manager has read all the books, attended all the seminars, and even has the t-shirt in the closet that reads "There is no I in team," which they proudly yet foolishly wear on staff in-service days. They stand about and like to toss out phrases like "leadership is about jumping out of a plane at 10,000 feet and building a parachute on the way down." I firmly believe that no one who parachutes will suggest that this strategy has actually worked. And even if a single occurrence did transpire, I am sure I would not suggest anyone try to repeat it. Getting lucky every once in while does not lead to improved professional practice.

Unfortunately, people follow the strong leader/weak manager blindly, like lemmings, because they offer an intoxicating charlatan's allure. They lead schools that appear to be performing very well while greatly exceeding the school's budget. They might bend the accounting rules or the approved human resources policies or ignore specific provisions of a collective agreement if they felt constrained by them. Deviating from agreed-to and accepted operating principles are not problems for them because they assume that there will always be more—more money, more staff, more time, more crafty management consultations or lawyers to confer with, just more everything—and they truly believe that their transgressions are warranted because their abilities exist without the need for any boundaries.

Strong Leader/Strong Manager

This is the administrator who does almost all things right but who has no illusion of perfection. The strong leader/strong manager sees that the necessary decisions that need to be made in a timely fashion are scheduled and happen on time, on budget, and to an acceptably high standard. Truly, this type of leader sees that the right people are hired and that they are supported professionally to develop as educators. But this leader also commits to deal with staff humanely and ethically and within the legal parameters even if they grossly underperform and her or his gut tells her or him to simply fire the person. As the matrix shown earlier illustrates, it is entirely possible for someone to be an excellent manager and leader. The gaze of this individual is more complete, focused both in an outward and an inward direction.

STRONG LEADERS LEAD WHILE MANAGING SKILLFULLY

While some people want to believe the school systems that have the most decentralized management systems, specifically site-based control over budgets and staffing, consistently outperform those divisions that are highly centralized, the truth is that such generalizations are much more myth than truth. As Michael Fullan, the former dean of the Ontario Institute for the Study of Education at the University of Toronto and a well-respected author of dozens of books on educational leadership, explains, the blind trust in decentralized approaches is an incomplete understanding of what the evidence indicates. In his book *Leadership and Sustainability: Systems Thinkers in Action*, Fullan advocates for a combined bottom-up (decentralized) and top-down (centralized) approach to operate schools and school systems effectively. Furthermore, in efforts to improve schools, one clear message has been learned from research: Neither complete centralization nor complete decentralization work. Centralization errs on the side of command and control (authoritarian rule), while decentralization errs toward idiosyncratic chaos (governed by self-interest). It is precisely somewhere between these two extremes where strong leaders/strong managers create physical and mental spaces that invite others to develop the programs and services that will allow students to flourish.

There really are only twenty-four hours in a day; no matter how well you divide up all of the waking hours you have, you cannot create more of them. No matter how much people want to believe in the illusion of being able to multitask and get everything done exceptionally well, the reality of administrative life is that there is only so much time and energy any one person can expend in a work day. If a principal is assiduously focused on the minutia of decentralized control, it comes at the expense of providing leadership about and for learning, neglecting the development of school-community networks.

The reality is that school systems must balance two competing needs: the need for efficiently managed school systems using consistent divisional standards that a centrally organized authority provides and the need for local principals to effectively lead a decision-making process while also being held responsible for the decision outcomes that impact their schools and local communities. School leaders need to not just strike a balance between managing and leading their schools but also find ways to maintain that balance once it is found to ensure their own well-being. Balancing any two responsibilities—as Archimedes's Law of the Lever teaches us—that are not exactly weighted the same for any period of time requires constant attention and dedicated effort and can be exhausting.

CONNECTING LOFTY VISIONS WITH STREET CREDIBILITY

Good leadership cannot do everything. Once we are prepared to admit it, we will recognize that some innovations will not work or at least they will not work well at the precise time we hoped for without a serious investment in changing the organization's existing culture, climate, and operating conditions. A fair number of "good ideas" that school leaders dream up at leader "retreats" or "visioning sessions" basically cannot get off the ground, not because someone has tethered them to the terra firma with the drivel of management problems, but because the current operating reality does not provide the atmospheric conditions required for them to take flight.

By way of analogy, I am going to suggest that what school leaders face is not very different from the dilemmas that many medical professionals face. It is becoming more and more common for someone in the health profession to develop a cutting-edge technological innovation or medical procedure that offers a glimmer of hope to someone inflicted with a terrible disease.

However, what the professionals must grapple with is whether to provide an expensive treatment or intervention that requires dozens of specialists for a single patient while incurring costs that might bring the health care system to the edge of bankruptcy, leaving it incapable of delivering basic health services to many, many others.

Unlike some functions of the health care system, for example the pharmaceuticals, for the most part, there are no venture capitalists waiting in the wings with deep-pocketed investors willing to take a risk with the hope of realizing a major return on investment. When educational initiatives are undertaken that are not financially sustainable, not legally permissible, or not respectful of the fact that taxpayers are not a bottomless well of money, then the fault of failing to launch the initiative or keep it afloat lies in a misguided understanding of what it means to lead schools.

While, arguably, managers are regarded as performing concrete daily tasks, such as overseeing deadlines, developing budgets, establishing structure within a team, and monitoring results, leaders are celebrated for developing visions for the future, creating team networks, and inspiring people to rise above challenges. It does not take much effort to see how these roles intertwine. While a leader is more associated with the world of ideas and a manager is associated with everyday reality, any school that wishes to succeed needs to employ a cadre of people who can dream even as they genuinely meet with the truths of the day.

Generally speaking, a lot of university-based educational administration or leadership preparation programs are structured and compartmentalized in such ways that they teach and present the vast majority of the challenges inherent in leading schools as discrete topics. This is not an indictment of educational administration programs. Truth be told, schools in general, and this is especially true as a child moves from elementary through middle school and into high school, are predicated on this same compartmentalization. In school, you do mathematics for an hour and then move on to English or maybe social studies, whether or not you are ready to stop thinking about mathematics. There is no great mystery to why schools compartmentalize knowledge: Academia in general likes to roll dice and sort information as a way of making sense of it, digging deep into it, and sharing it.

Universities are fragmented and siloed with business faculties occupying state-of-the-art executive centers, law faculties located close to green spaces that offer the aura of serenity, and colleges of education placed in circa-1960 architectural cement block buildings. Knowledge is equally delineated, with specialized courses taught only to those who are entitled to learn their secrets.

Businesses are similarly compartmentalized with certain divisions or departments. This is typically based on theoretical and technical expertise, but is also divided in terms of the organizational structure. For example, the human resources experts are almost always separated from the legal ones, who in turn are physically separated from the finance folks. There is a demarcation among the individuals who are responsible for specific activities, and these activities happen at different times and in different places. They exercise dominion over their specialized knowledge.

However, this contrived structuralism does not, in fact, represent how most people think and learn. Knowledge is an interconnected web of information and insight, which sometimes leads to wisdom with no subject boundaries and no grade levels. Most people seem to agree that if a learner wants to pursue an interest in something, it should be possible, with no mind to whether or not it is part of somebody else's agenda, which subject heading it fits under, or in which grade it should be studied.

Regardless of how it is spoken or written about, administrative life rarely proceeds in a compartmentalized fashion. The day-to-day work of a school administrator, from vice principal through to the chief superintendent, is made up of interrelated, complex issues and challenges that rarely arrive in such a way that they can be dealt with in a linear manner. Educational administrators do not have the luxury of segmenting their days so that they can have one hour to devote to a contentious legal issue and then as the clock's minute hand hits twelve open up the "books" to reconcile a wonky budget before moving on in the following hour to deal with a festering personnel challenge, after which they can sit back and leisurely eat their lunches. In the fast-paced problem-solving and decision-making reality of the principalship, it is clear that most facets of administrative life are inter-connected.

It is not easy being responsible for the business operations (or management functions) of schools these days, and it is definitely not regarded as glamorous work. In this era of heightened expectations, administrators are assumed to possess both professional and technical expertise. Although there are exhortations for principals to be instructional and ethical leaders, very often they see themselves as being saddled with many of the same tasks that one hundred years ago Henri Fayol labeled as the "POSDCORB" functions of administration: namely Planning, Organizing, Staffing, Directing, Co-Ordinating, Reporting, and Budgeting. Regrettably, they see these as the anchors that limit their leadership potential.

BREATHING SPACE

Imagine yourself eavesdropping on the following conversation at a wine and cheese reception for newly hired school principals and vice principals:

"What do you think is the steepest part of the learning curve in assuming your first principalship?" asked of one the new vice principals, somewhat starstruck at simply being invited to the event, while anticipating the next round of hors d'oeuvres.

"Probably remembering what all the letters mean in 'P-O-S-D-C-O-R-B' when we have to write the leadership certificate exam," replied the equally newly appointed principal with deadpan and arrogant delivery.

"Really, there is an exam?" questioned the vice principal, who is now more interested in the complimentary wine than the conversation. "Did you just make that up?"

The point is that while your new acquaintances may just smile and eat some more crab canapés, the reality is that if you or they flounder while enacting any one of those functions, your staff—who did not get invited to the event—may publicly admit what they may have been thinking since the email announcement appeared in their inbox announcing your administrative appointment, which is: "He (or she) is in way over his (or her) head, and we are in serious trouble this year!"

FOCUS ON THE NEEDS OF FOLLOWERS

Even though the draw of leadership is strong, if you ask anyone who has done the work, they will say it is not easy to be a school leader, especially if you consider a fundamental question of leadership, which is: "Why would anyone follow me?" It takes followers to be considered a leader. An individual who blazes a trail into the unknown is not considered a leader unless someone, anyone, is willing to follow. And willingness to follow is key. You do not get to call yourself a "leader" because individuals are compelled to listen to you or lose their jobs.

True enough, it takes courage to step up to lead, but no one will follow if you are neither leading for the right reasons nor heading in a direction that they trust you can take them while maintaining the solvency of the organization. As much as teaching is a vocation, most folks still want to get paid or be held legally liable for someone else's errors. They want to follow leaders who are skillful managers.

The two functions of leading and managing begin to converge when a principal manages by marshaling the necessary resources that will support the important ideas that improve the likelihood that students will succeed. Teachers, staff, and parents want to follow individuals who go about picking the right battles to fight to see that that collective vision can become real.

If you want to get the best performance out of your staff, you need to be excellent in what you actually do and not just in what you think. Few expect perfection. But many are willing to follow individuals who work hard in their attempts to build the structural conditions that might really allow staff and students to achieve excellence in teaching and learning.

There is a saying in human resource management that talent seeks out other talent. Education is no different. Talented teachers want to work with other talented teachers, and they all want to work with talented school leaders who can expand their worlds and make them better at the teaching and learning dynamic. They want to trust in the capacity of those they follow. Being worthy of followership—an element of trustworthiness—is grounded in a belief that the person leading and managing holds the qualities outlined in figure 1.3.

These principals, the ones who do not take the trust their staff places in them for granted, understand the business of schooling and use that insight to help others see more than what is simply in front of their immediate sightlines.

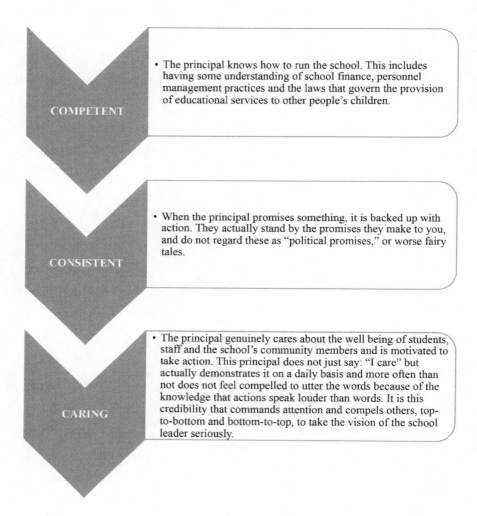

COMPETENT
- The principal knows how to run the school. This includes having some understanding of school finance, personnel management practices and the laws that govern the provision of educational services to other people's children.

CONSISTENT
- When the principal promises something, it is backed up with action. They actually stand by the promises they make to you, and do not regard these as "political promises," or worse fairy tales.

CARING
- The principal genuinely cares about the well being of students, staff and the school's community members and is motivated to take action. This principal does not just say: "I care" but actually demonstrates it on a daily basis and more often than not does not feel compelled to utter the words because of the knowledge that actions speak louder than words. It is this credibility that commands attention and compels others, top-to-bottom and bottom-to-top, to take the vision of the school leader seriously.

Figure 1.3.   Leadership Credibility

This kind of leadership requires individuals who can consistently put into practice their principles. They keep their eyes open for the staff's professional interests, abilities, and willingness to professionally grow because those undiscovered abilities and interests might well be where teachers will ultimately find their underlying capacities to move the school forward. Principals who lead and manage make plans to enhance the services and programs that students need to succeed at school without losing sight of the fact that these commitments require money now and over the long haul. Sustainability is neither a fad nor a curricular add-on. It is part of their way of thinking and creating school plans.

Obviously, they need to take some risks. But they calculate the costs associated with the risks not just to themselves but also to others who might be affected by the decisions. In short, effective school leaders see what others cannot see because they are constantly looking for it. They push their people to a level that perhaps a staff could not envision on its own. However, in pushing and pulling their colleagues, they work tirelessly to create the requisite conditions that allow everyone to find success. They allow others to reap the rewards of their vision as a result. And yes, leaders follow rules.

I have heard a well-paid speaker and author suggest that leaders should break all the rules. I do not agree, especially because my experience is that sometimes all that the most vulnerable members in society have to protect them are the rules. The rule breakers also seem to correspond with the weaker managers. Of course, when the rules are not working or are limiting the school's ability to meet the needs of all the students, effective leaders work to change the rules and, from time to time, accept deviations and mistakes as the rare exceptions, provided they stem from the right intentions and do not cause others who need protection harm. Rules that work should indeed guide and define practice.

Great managers look inward. They look inside the organization, into each individual's capacity to commit to the organization's mission, into the differences in style, goals, needs, and motivation of each person. But they also, by contrast, look outward. They look out at the future and search out all available and alternative routes forward. They focus on broad patterns, finding connections and cracks, and then press home their advantage where the resistance is weakest. Though it seems that cultivating the outward gaze is in vogue, the equally important inward gaze on the business operations of schools will give a school principal the 360-degree vision they actually need to create the conditions where students have the highest likelihood of finding success.

SUMMARY

Hopefully I have convinced you that it is entirely possible for a person to be a brilliant manager and a terrible leader. Moreover, it is just as imaginable for a person to excel as a leader and fail as a manager. In some regards, it is not his or her fault. The books and well-paid consultants have indoctrinated him or her to believe it is an "either/or" proposition.

I would like to challenge that orthodoxy because there are some individuals who excel at both, and regardless of what you might think Lady Gaga means, they were not "born that way." They worked hard and are committed to learning how to effectively lead and manage and have succeeded. It is this heterodoxy of both leadership and management that school communities require to thrive nowadays.

This text is therefore written in a manner that presents the topics of personnel management, finance, and risk management in a way that demonstrates the interconnectedness of each function as a matter of both leading and managing the business operations of schools. It is not meant to further problematize the work of school administrators more than the work already is. I know how hard the work is. Rather, the text is written and structured to illustrate, elucidate, and, hopefully, illuminate the complexity involved in leading and managing schools in challenging times so that principals and vice principals will recognize the critical importance of considering the effects of providing both—leadership and management—in each and every decision they make.

Chapter Two

Leadership Principles and Practices for Personnel Management

The key is to keep company only with people who uplift you, whose presence calls forth your best.
—Epictetus, a Greek Stoic philosopher during the first century AD

Ample research and workplace evidence suggests what many already know: Having just a few lazy or incompetent characters around the staff room can ruin the performance of a team or an entire organization, no matter how stellar the other employees may be. Bad characters and poor performers distract and drag everyone down, and their lack of motivation and commitment can be remarkably contagious even to some of those who would otherwise be motivated and engaged. School leaders who hire new staff who have not clearly demonstrated the capacity to succeed as educators—perhaps because the leader believes he or she can miraculously turn them into star performers—may feed their own egos and on rare occasions find a successful turnaround, but more often than not set the stage for sheer disappointment when the newly hired project fails.

BREATHING SPACE

There is a politically insensitive human resource joke that is frequently used by conference keynote speakers who stand at well-worn and off-colored laminate lecterns in outdated tailored polyester suits in poorly lit hotel conference ballrooms and attempt to be funny. The joke goes something like this: When a doctor makes a surgical mistake, tragically and all too often, a patient dies. After some soul-searching the doctor is forced to move on. When a defense attorney makes a trial error, which unfortunately happens from time to time, an innocent goes to jail and the lawyer is forced to move on but usually with a little less soul-searching than the surgeon. When a school principal, however, makes a hiring mistake, which by the way no one ever admits to, the mistake says "Good morning" each and every day to a class full of students who are forced to endure the mistake for a whole year. Principals, it is purported, prefer to not expend energy searching their souls for solace; it's considered to be way too emotionally burdensome. Conference attendees laugh, at least slightly, as they lean uncomfortably close to the person sitting beside them, squirm slightly, and remark, "It was a good joke, wasn't it?" Many of them, however, are not willing to admit to those same newly found colleagues that they, in fact, work with a "mistake" who "someone else" hired.

- **PRINCIPLE 2.1:** *Know why you exist as a social organization: It's about teaching and learning.*
- **PRACTICE 2.1:** *Focus your leadership efforts on getting the very best people into positions that support the teaching and learning dynamic so students can succeed.*

SEARCHING FOR AND DEVELOPING TALENT

Leadership, regardless of the industry, is very much about hiring the most talented people possible to fill the available job openings. Personnel leadership, however, specifically in education, has a heightened importance as it focuses on the functional aspects of recruiting, selecting, placing, professionally developing, evaluating, and compensating the gifted ones who will be granted almost unfettered access to children. Personnel leadership is about diligently screening and selecting those individuals who will hold the public's trust to teach children. It is important to remember that formal education, namely schooling, is a public good enabled by public or private institutions operating squarely within the public sphere within which various dependence relations are constituted, including relations of both trust and reliance. The public trusts and relies on school leaders to use their management insight to find only the most talented, capable, and competent adults to be trusted as teachers. This is a trust that should never be taken for granted and needs to be earned day in and day out.

Debates about what constitute the prized goals of education continue. And to some degree such debates are the fabric of a healthy democracy. However, nurturing student success, which is the central aim of formal schooling regardless of how it is defined and assessed, ought to be closed to debate. While it is important to note that schools do not exist in a vacuum and that there are a tremendous number of out-of-school factors that affect a child's ability to succeed academically, one thing that is known is that the quality of the educational workforce is the primary in-school determinant of whether or not students will achieve success.

Since the publication of Jim Collins's *Good to Great: Why Some Companies Make the Leap—and Others Don't* back in 2001, it has generally become accepted that the most important decision that leaders in complex organizations make are not "what" decisions but rather "who" decisions. Decades of studies on the determinants of student achievement highlight the fact that "good" or "effective" teachers, however those terms are defined, have a tremendous impact on student success. There is overwhelming agreement that of the many in-school factors that contribute to student achievement, the single most impactful variable is the effectiveness of the teachers who they learn from and with. The "who" matters not only in deciding the "what" of schooling in terms of a program of studies, but it is also the collective "who" of the school's staff that provides a tangible meaning to a student's experience of attending. Over and over, students suggest that, for better mostly but sometimes for worse, teachers make a profound difference to their in-school success.

Thus, focusing energy, effort, and resources on personnel leadership efforts on the dynamic relationship that exists between teaching and learning is, in fact, the single most potent factor that school leaders can influence. While it might seem trivial, educators ought to focus their leadership efforts on helping students develop the intellectual, emotional, psychological, and social competencies that will allow them to fully participate in civil society and flourish as human beings. This can be done through a disciplined commitment to attract, recruit, professionally develop, and retain the most competent cadre of educators and support staff that is possible. The effects—positive or negative—that teachers, teaching assistants, and principals can have on students can be profound and lasting.

Without having the best people to work in the system, there is no "what" because the "what" represents learning outcomes. This may seem obvious, especially as it is read from the safe distance of a desk, but principals and superintendents often waste time trying to fix the process of the "what"—like fixating on whether or not they ought to allow to students to bring their own devices to school or whether or not school beautification projects increase student engagement or whether or not ball caps impede learning—when in fact their ability to hire and employ the right person makes the biggest difference as to whether or not students will find success in school. For the record, while there is no empirical evidence to suggest that the wearing of hats insulates the brain against learning, volumes of research concludes that ineffective educators most certainly cost students learning opportunities.

While obvious to name, it is sometimes taken for granted by school administrators that the most fundamental building block of schoolwide success is a result of focusing the spotlight on personnel leadership to find the individuals with the right competencies, skills, and dispositions for each and every job within the organization. Besides the immediate satisfaction of working with a cadre of talented people, a commitment to make personnel leadership a priority sends a message throughout the organization and to all of its external stakeholder groups: I am dedicated to surrounding my students with the very best people I can so that they can succeed; full stop.

- **PRINCIPLE 2.2:** *Harness the talent and passion of the current staff to support learning.*
- **PRACTICE 2.2:** *Challenge your staffs' intellect, unleash their passions, and engage their imaginations in pursuit of teaching effectiveness.*

Effective personnel leaders explore the talents and passions to educate that exist within the school's staff. They recognize that "deep teaching smarts" may be obscured at times and therefore look beyond what seems apparent but maybe only exists at the surface level to discover the capabilities that each person has within the organization. When the talents and passions of the staff are allowed to serve the mission of the school, students and staff will flourish.

How does the practice of this look? You might explicitly

- give your staff permission to think, speak, and act with intentionality on matters that involve making sustainable improvements to the teaching and learning dynamic;
- provide them with opportunities to contribute to a school culture fixated on student success;
- encourage everyone to ask hard questions about how best to support student learning and then search for possible answers; and
- create processes that nurture people's strengths while providing them with opportunities to work on their weaknesses.

Realizing that each staff member has strengths enables you to leverage these strengths into productive and rewarding work for him or her and the school community. At the same time, allowing people to work on their weaknesses, whether self-identified or ones you have noted, typically stimulates professional growth and encourages engagement.

Work collectively as a staff to find a level of agreement on the kinds of knowledge, skills, and dispositions that characterize what it means to teach effectively in your local context. Lots of books exist that describe teaching effectiveness, and while some offer valuable insight, others do not. As a community of educators committed to effective professional practice, it should be required that everyone reads a few. In case they balk, remind them that we do not give students the option to not read because we fundamentally think it will support and encourage them to learn. Offer opportunities to meet, discuss, and challenge the ideas that are presented in the learning materials. Revise, amend, and shape the initial ideas that surface into a working concept or a few working concepts of what effective teaching might be in the local context. But get agreement to work with that initial framework to develop a sense of what effective teaching practice constitutes.

In simple terms, if you do not have a clear picture of what constitutes effective teaching, even if only in your mind, you are not likely to know "it" when you see "it." This connects back to the truth of the epigraph that opened this chapter. Far too many principals claim they know "it" when they see "it" but do not have much more than a vague idea of what "it" means in terms of highly effective teaching practice. When pressed, these same principals resort to the gated discourses of educational leadership, which can sometimes sound like "edu-babble," and suggest they are looking for a "team player" without spending any time thinking about and outlining for themselves what it means to "play" on the team or what the goal of the team actually is. Others hide behind the silliness of suggesting that it is impossible to describe effective teaching because it comes down to personal "style" without acknowledging the truth that style without substance is meaningless.

Based on the initial framework, work with your staff to collectively develop a "profile" of what effective teaching practice is in a school or in a divisional context. Collaboratively and deliberatively, which is the opposite of the sometimes haphazard processes that currently exist, and using input from other principals, teachers, central office administrators, and maybe even students and parents, develop some broad categories and criteria that highlight the kinds of required knowledge, skills, and attributes to be an effective teacher. It is difficult, but strive to find agreement on the knowledge, skills, and dispositions that characterize effective teachers. Use clear language to describe the observable qualities of teachers who are regarded by their colleagues, students, and parents as being masterful in their professional practice. This is a critical step in developing a sense of what it takes and what it means to effectively teach. This profile should connect with an idealized notion of what effective teaching means for a specific school and division. Be honest when some people begin to feel inadequate as they hold themselves up to such a high standard. It is not about our failure to be perfect but rather about articulating a sense of what teachers need to know and need to be able to do to be the best educators they can be.

The process forces school administrators to sketch out on paper, not just in their minds, what "it" is and to encourage the school community to shape their ideas. It provides the school community with the opportunity to commit to paper what they expect to see or hear in an effective teacher's classroom. It allows them to have a working idea of what they believe the culture of teaching in that particular context is all about.

- **PRINCIPLE 2.3:** *Commit to make the staff you have become even better at the teaching and learning dynamic.*
- **PRACTICE 2.3:** *Invest time, money, and energy in professional development initiatives that make lasting improvements to student learning efforts.*

The most powerful strategy school systems and schools have at their disposal to improve teacher effectiveness is professional development. Deep understandings of students, the contexts they come from, and both the theories and practices that support student learning are required by educators at all levels of the K–12 system. It seems fairly evident: The quality of an education system cannot exceed the quality of its teachers and support staff.

Professional development initiatives will only be as effective as the learning outcomes they intend to support. Having a clear picture of what the intended learning outcomes will be and how these outcomes will lead to improved student success is imperative. Far too much time and energy, not to mention money, is devoted to workshops intended as "awareness" or "exposure" campaigns that have little to no demonstrable impact on supporting student efforts to reach their learning goals. Instead, professional development needs to be centrally oriented to leverage the kind of professional practice that will lead to improvements in student learning.

The steepest part of the learning curve is not learning new approaches to teaching but rather in understanding how to implement the theories into practice. One of the primary reasons why so much professional development is considered to be ineffective is because teachers do not believe that they are supported during the implementation phase. In the same way that learning to drive a car safely cannot be done behind the comfort of a desk alone, actually employing a teaching strategy in the classroom is more difficult than simply learning the strategy. Failing to provide "at-the-elbow" support reduces the implementation rates of new ideas, creates a disservice to teachers who would like to improve, and arouses the skepticism of the public who have invested in supporting their professional development.

"If you don't know where you are going, any road will take you there," observed the Cheshire Cat in Lewis Carroll's *Alice in Wonderland*. It is also true in designing a professional growth plan for teachers. If you have not developed a framework—even just a general one—of what constitutes effective teaching, then it is impracticable to recommend how a teacher might embark on the journey of developing professionally.

PURPOSEFUL PROFESSIONAL DEVELOPMENT

By way of a metaphor, what follows is an illustrative example. Admittedly it is a rather simplistic example but one that hopefully makes a clear point. Imagine that there are three doors in different colors located right front of you. Other than the color of each door, in all other respects they look exactly the same. Each door represents a possible choice for the direction of a teacher's professional growth. You are given the choice to open only one door each year. And by the way, in order for you to open the door, your employer must pay a thousand dollars upfront—no returns and no exchanges. Hopefully, for that reason alone, you have some clue what lies behind the door.

Each door leads somewhere, that much is true. Once opened, the teacher is required to step through the doorway and must step fully across the threshold so as to allow it to close behind her or him. You have committed the teacher to the journey for the entire school year.

As a reference point for this metaphoric reference, consider the idea of "way finding." In simple terms, way finding includes the various ways in which people orient themselves in physical space and navigate from place to place. One example of a way finder that can be used to guide the professional development of teachers, but obviously not the only one, as suggested by respected scholars Linda Darling-Hammond and her colleague John Bransford is that effective teachers share some of the characteristics shown in figure 2.1 as an example of one conceptual model of effective teaching.

The model is intended to be an illustrative example and not the declarative statement on what effective teaching must be. It does, however, provide a target, and if you do not know where you are headed—in other words you outright dismiss that there are markers that distinguish effective from ineffective teaching practices—then allowing teachers to step through any doorway of professional development will suffice, even if that so-called learning journey takes them nowhere in reality.

Many educational leaders follow the "any door" philosophy and not only permit but also promote the fairy tale that any professional development journey is worthwhile. They believe that there is a chance that one door might open up and reveal some wonderfully joyous path that will be the start of an amazing learning adventure. Concomitantly, they dismiss the probability that it might just as likely open into a bog—the knee-deep putrid muck of a swamp that drains a teacher's energy as she or he slogs through it with no dry land in sight. Such approaches are exhausting.

The reason for using doors in this analogy rather than the notion of choices is because, when people have a number of choices put in front of them, they tend to choose a bit of one and a bit of another. But professional life does not really work that way. With respect to professional development, the key is choosing a direction that develops some specific teaching compe-

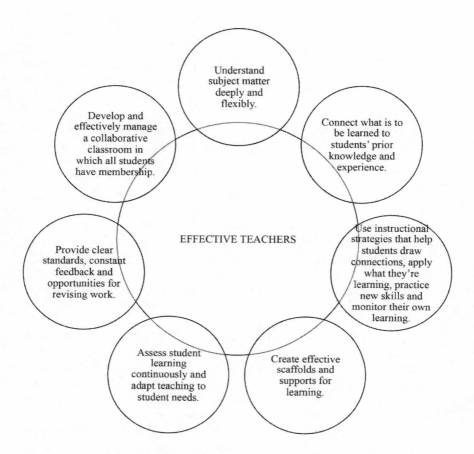

Figure 2.1. Characteristics of Effective Teachers

tencies and specifically the ones that are in need of greatest improvement and then committing to a professional development plan that has the greatest likelihood of arriving at the destination. It is about stepping through the most appropriate door and being confident as it closes behind that, of the limited choices, this is the most important path to follow.

Change requires time and ongoing support. There is a need to provide on-the-job professional support, be it through mentors, coaches, professional learning communities, or supportive working teams that will help educators when they inevitably experience challenges, but also take advantage of the opportunities to make a positive difference for students. And sometimes useful external expertise can be found in colleges and faculties of education, professional associations, and other organizations that can reinforce professional development.

Professional development needs to be driven by what students need in order to succeed rather than loosely connected to what principals and teachers think they want. The time and financial investment made for effective professional development impacts both the educator and the student. Principals, vice principals, teachers, and educational assistants need to take collective responsibility for all students' success to ensure that effective practices move from classroom to classroom and school to school. Teachers support effective school leaders, and effective school leaders are essential to move successful system- and schoolwide student-centered professional learning initiatives forward.

- **PRINCIPLE 2.4:** *Hire the very best for all positions and at all times.*
- **PRACTICE 2.4:** *Where you are lacking the staff you need, actively recruit and select the people with the requisite knowledge, skills, and dispositions necessary to ensure the current and future learning needs of students are met.*

The tendency in teacher hiring is to focus on only the immediate needs of the school. Teacher hiring, however, ought to also take a longer, more strategic view that extends beyond the current need to fill a vacancy with a person and instead include a perspective that a teacher hired today will not only teach this generation of young people but also the next one. Hiring is not only potentially a thirty-year financial commitment to pay someone a salary. It is also an expression of confidence that the person hired is not just excellent for the needs of today's students but is also going to be great for students whose parents may not even be born yet.

There are a lot of pressures that come with leadership in contemporary schools. The list of items of what a school principal must accomplish—legally and morally speaking—seems to be ever expanding, and there does not appear to be a sign that this pressure will be lessening in the near future. It is worth reminding readers not to lose sight of the obvious: even though the public's expectations thrust on superintendents, principals, and vice principals seem to be ever expanding, giving a large amount of focus to the hiring of effective teachers matters. It matters a lot. All things considered, the public has no appetite for incompetence in the classroom or for those who place incompetent teachers in front of students.

While some people take for granted the power of the advertisements to create an engaging narrative, most marketing professionals would disagree. Create job advertisements that attract the educators you want to work with and pique their interest in what your school has to offer. In the advertisement, describe what it means to be an educator committed to serving the needs of students and the local school community, and finally convince those who believe they match the description to apply by providing clear directions on how to do so.

In the end, the most lasting mark any school principal can make on a school community is the quality of staff hired by that principal. Hiring the best possible candidates for each and every position makes a long-term difference to school and division quality, and arguably more importantly, it makes a lasting difference to student success. Even with the latest gadgets at their disposal, students will not learn without the guidance of a talented teacher.

Hiring teachers who are ineffective or not well suited for the hard work that teaching entails hurts, and it can do so in lasting and profound ways. Students who are fortunate to be assigned an effective teacher can exceed the learning outcomes for the year; students who suffer under an ineffective teacher lose almost the entire year's worth of educational opportunity. The learning difference for students who are taught by the very best teachers versus the students who toil under the very worst can be as large as two years' worth of learning outcomes. This difference is too large to ignore and too significant to leave to unfounded hiring practices.

- **PRINCIPLE 2.5:** *Some things matter more, a lot more, in hiring than do other things.*
- **PRACTICE 2.5:** *Ensure that the people and processes involved in hiring decisions have been carefully selected to do the work.*

When we "make do" with what we have when it comes to teacher recruitment and selection practices, we set up a culture of hiring that will, at best, result in mediocrity and, at worse, fail children. What an admission of the disservice we do to ourselves, to our staff, and, most importantly, to our students when we settle for "two feet and a heartbeat."

In the book *Infoglut: How Too Much Information Is Changing the Way We Think and Know*, Mark Andrejeviv makes the compelling case that a hallmark of our time is the fact that we are surrounded by data smog, which is an expression for the sludge and muck that gets pushed out in the information age in which we live. And those charged with the responsibility of collecting useful information to screen and select new teachers are not, in fact, immune to the pathogenic effect of this smog. Information overload in the hiring process, specifically to the point where there is so much information that it is no longer effective to use it to make decisions, affects principals and superintendents as much as everyone else.

The end result of all-inclusive assessments of potential teaching effectiveness that do not allow decision makers to focus their attention on those factors that research suggests ought to count most in hiring decisions is that decision makers become distracted by marginal pieces of information that not only draw attention away from the most reliable information but also obscure it from sight.

It takes effort and resources to hire well and find the best. Effective hiring does not require a complicated system; however, it does require one that is complex enough to wade through the "almost good enough to be teachers" pile to find the most talented and gifted candidates. Hiring the best possible candidates makes a long-term difference to school and division quality and, most importantly, to student learning. By increasing student learning, good teachers gradually improve any division and often help improve their fellow teachers as well by pushing the professional conversation that colleagues engage in to deeper understandings of what constitutes effective teaching and learning practices.

Hiring well requires a thoughtful and deliberate approach that reflects the best practices of human resources management and an investment of time and money to ensure that those charged with finding the best know what they are doing. It requires a principled and practiced approach to hiring. Even when we embark on solving the problems we created with poor hiring practices, we are left with unwanted effects that can take years to abate. Teacher dismissal due to poor hiring threatens program continuity and parent confidence in the school and negatively impacts student beliefs in their abilities to be successful at school. Yes, it is possible to get rid of terrible teachers with enough effort and commitment to a fair process, but in their wake we are left with scores of children whose learning has been deleteriously affected. In the long run, hiring well is much easier than firing.

Few are willing to acknowledge it, but not everyone who wants to hire teachers or wants to be involved in the hiring process is actually good at it. Providing instructional leadership, a critical concern for school leaders, is a distinctively different skill based on distinctively different knowledge from what is required to screen and select teachers. While targeted professional development and training focused on developing capacity in the human resource function can support the growth of principals and vice principals, the truth is that not everyone has the personal disposition to be effective in making hiring decisions. Screening and selecting is tough work and it requires a bit of a cold heart to tell those who feel destined to be a teacher that they cannot teach, or at least cannot teach for you. You may feel sympathetic toward the candidate, who in response to the question of "Why do you want to be a teacher?" replies, "My parents were teachers, their parents were teachers, and all I have ever wanted to do is be a teacher." Wanting to do something professionally—like singing, acting, playing sports, or teaching— does not automatically mean someone will be talented at it.

The reality is that the best indicator of someone who is effective at teacher screening and selection is a track record of successful hiring, and developing a track record requires professional development, guided practice, and time.

- Decide who will interview the candidates based on their proven competency to interview and hire well.
- Provide them with time and resources to further develop their capacity in human resources management.
- Ensure that interviewers focus on the evidence presented in the application and review the necessarily subjective interpretations they made of the material they have reviewed.

It is not easy to look a person in the eyes and honestly respond, "That may be true, but from what you have demonstrated, you will not be teaching here," but sometimes it needs to be said. And not everyone has the ability or emotional fortitude to say it.

Human resources professionals employ a variety of well-researched recruitment and selection techniques that are designed to increase the likelihood of finding the right person for the right job. Many principals and superintendents sadly lack the training and/or access to the human resource management tools that could better equip them to complete the most important administrative task they are responsible to do: recruit and select effective teachers for each and every classroom. Instead, they are left to figure it out on the job—a kind of trial-by-fire approach. While it might be uncomfortable for them to admit, most principals are willing to take on the hiring responsibility without any formal training. Those same principals, however, would recoil at the very thought of allowing untrained adults to have access to children in classrooms as teachers. It is a paradox that they go about hiring only those qualified to teach without any specific training in human resource management or effective hiring themselves. Commit to use contemporary research and evidence-based hiring practices designed for schools or other public sector agencies that are aligned with the goal of hiring the best.

In 1830, George Combe, one of England's most prominent phrenologists, explained that he could tell if a prospective servant was conscientious or untrustworthy by examining the bumps and bulges on his head. While it might sound sort of creepy, imagine if such a process were used to hire teachers today and what the results—beyond lawsuits—might be. We would all like to believe that personnel selection approaches have evolved a lot since the nineteenth century. But if the research on the hiring practices of schools and school divisions tells us anything with certainty, it is that we ought to question just how far schools and systems have really come from hiring based on a host of superstitious beliefs that lack any predictive validity to ensuring that the most promising candidates get hired. While far from a definitive list of all of the kinds of considerations that should be made in careful, school-centric workforce planning, the following list of unwritten rules warrants thoughtful consideration by anyone who hopes to align hiring decisions with the strategic priorities of a school.

Schools are constantly undergoing significant changes such as increased pressure for inclusion, the need to offer programming for an increasingly diverse student demographic, and the rapidity of technological enhancements to program delivery. Therefore with any vacancy there should be a thoughtful and thorough job analysis that does not just look at the immediate needs of the school or division but also looks into the future and tries to predict what might be needed in the teachers for the next generation of students and not just the present ones. This fundamentally important first step requires that school administrators sketch out on paper what "it" looks and sounds like in their schools. What does highly effective teaching look like or sound like when it is observed in that specific school? The purpose is not to reduce teaching to an itemized list of skills but to create a vivid picture on paper of what it takes to be a highly successful teacher for the school or division.

Determine what kinds of evidence are required in application packages and then carefully screen the applicants against these, choosing only those who present evidence that has been measured as meeting or exceeding the standards that were developed earlier in a local framework for effective teaching. For example, is cultural competence as important as subject matter preparation for a particular hire? In some contexts, it might be impossible to teach without cultural competence and the otherwise capable teacher will fail. In another instance, a strong subject matter specialist who is fairly clueless about cultural competence may be a detriment to learning.

Following the same process outlined earlier to develop the screening criteria and framework for effective teaching, develop behaviorally based interview questions and a rubric for assessing the quality of candidates' answers. All too often personnel committees forget that developing and agreeing on what constitutes an acceptable response is as important as developing the question.

Review interview perceptions and assessments of the candidates, compare these to the evidence collected in the applications and interviews, and triangulate all of the data. Do not only focus on what you think was said, but rather develop a composite image of the candidate using the totality of the evidence by looking for what is consistent and where there are discrepancies in the information collected.

Complete detailed and thorough background checks, which include employment and education verifications, to ensure that what they said they have done they actually did. It is common for individuals to manage their résumés and from time to time inflate their qualifications and/or experience. Reference checks should be used to confirm or disconfirm information provided and/or validate the opinions that the interview team formed about the "most likely to be hired" of the prospective candidates.

Finally, as the final selection is made, take care to ensure that the process of screening and selection is indeed related to a candidate's preparedness to be an effective teacher, does not violate the candidate's rights, and is not solely based on the inherent biases and preferences we all carry about the types of people we enjoy working with as colleagues. In short, it is not about whom we enjoy as company but rather who is best suited to help children learn exceptionally well.

In addition to the effects on student learning, what those same teachers who get hired bring to their place of employment impacts the level of professionalism, collaboration, and trust within the school's culture. As schools and divisions work to develop a cohort of highly effective teachers to improve the educational opportunities of students, it is important to note that those same employment practices set the stage for the initial socialization into a professionally led organization that takes employee hiring very seriously.

Regrettably, far too many principals and superintendents who talk about the importance of hiring the very best candidates repeatedly employ very weak human resource practices because they have always done it that way. For these school leaders, it seems as if repeating the same act over and over again without knowing if it yields the best results is a "good enough" human resource strategy.

Let us begin with a simple premise: If a school or division is serious about hiring the very best, its leadership must agree on the importance of effective teacher selection, and all who participate in the process must be committed to the task no matter how hard or time consuming it might be to revise current practices. It requires all of those who lead and manage schools to commit to the process to make it work.

School board members must say that they want the best teachers throughout the school division and then commit to it. This does not imply that they should be involved in hiring teachers and staff. But if they are serious about getting the best, then they need to invest the already limited pool of money into improving the hiring process so that superintendents, principals, and vice principals can become better at hiring. A zero-dollar investment will always result in a zero-sum return on investment no matter what they try to spin to the public.

Superintendents should publicly emphasize the priority of choosing who is involved in making hiring decisions and should then provide the necessary mentorship and resources so they can carry it out. The focus on hiring the best teachers and staff needs to be a year-round commitment and not an endeavor relegated to conversation and a flurry of activity in the late February through May time period like so many school divisions do.

Teachers should call for the best colleagues to be placed in the classrooms next to theirs. Teachers should not be passive about having to accept working shoulder to shoulder with poor performers. Recall that talent seeks talent. Teachers who believe they work with exceptionally talented colleagues tend to commit more time and energy.

This is not an open invitation to involve parents in the actual mechanics of a specific hiring decision. It is fair to suggest that almost every parent wants what they believe is best for their child, and this is not always what is necessarily best for all children. That is why parents should not sit on hiring committees for their child's class. But that said, parents should be offered a chance to voice their preferences in general terms about the kind of people they want teaching their children. It respects their role in the teaching and learning dynamic and engages them in important policy decisions.

Finally, principals and vice principals need to be willing to provide as much of their time as is necessary to find exceptional teacher candidates. They cannot be content to learn personnel leadership through practice. All twenty years of bad hiring practices results in is a whole lot of bad hires and suffering students. Principals and vice principals need to think critically about their own capabilities in hiring and seek out resources—workshops, courses, books, and/or mentors—who can support their growth as personnel leaders.

It is a long list and a hefty commitment that has been suggested, but truth be told, without the collective commitment and energy of the school community writ large, the results of any improvement in staff hiring will be incomplete at best. However, imagine the results and the increase in public confidence if we truly did commit ourselves to searching for the most talented individuals to work in schools and engaged our communities to help in some manner in the hunt for those great educators.

Those responsible for hiring should consider division and school goals when discussing the need for new teachers: strong classroom performers, teachers who meet student needs and priorities, visible gains among different types of learning, and flexible innovators who adapt to change and respond to challenges. Different groups—that is, teachers, board members, and administrators—should initiate these discussions among themselves and with each other. Parental input should be welcomed. The folks who work in formal leadership roles should recognize that upset feelings and temporary disturbances are a regular part of the hiring process—such as when some are asked to contribute but not others—and may want to adopt a set of principles of good hiring. Finally, the division should elucidate its most outstanding qualities in personnel leadership and management, namely that it currently employs best practices, which are focused on remarkable hiring results and reflect common ideals of what it means to work with children.

It was suggested earlier that experience in and of itself does not lead to improved practice. Professional development and training, however, can dramatically improve the competence and reliability of interviewers to interview well. Without training and support, well-intentioned interviewers may unwittingly perpetuate ineffective interview habits, may not ask questions that solicit the kind of useful information they want and need, and may even ask questions that violate an interviewee's human rights. Additionally, because teachers are hired for both a school and a division, those involved in the hiring process should have a reasonably comprehensive understanding of the specific needs of a school and also possess an awareness of the division's educational priorities targeted at systemwide school improvement, which inevitably are to be enacted by teachers, including those newly hired.

Taken together, this suggests that those hiring committee members charged with teacher hiring should first be screened and selected using a rigorous process; schools need to set a goal of selecting those who will be the best at hiring before they embark on filling an opening. Once chosen, any hiring committee members need to be provided with appropriately aligned professional development in human resources management. Similarly to Jim Collins, Michael Fullan has also suggested that strategic workforce planning is ultimately about having the right people, with the right knowledge, skills, and dispositions, at the right places, doing the right things at the right times so that children can learn exceptionally well. This sentiment seems to hold equally true for those who are charged with the responsibility of finding exceptional or even just excellent teachers to hire if we agree that settling for excellent might be good enough.

Teacher hiring can be either centralized at the division office, conducted independently by each school, or be a hybrid of both centralized tasks and decentralized tasks. The perspectives and needs of the central office often differ greatly from local concerns, thereby affecting the selection process. For example, some schools might not understand the seemingly lengthy time line of central screening procedures, which can frustrate and discourage applicants. While many school administrators are focused on the immediate needs of their school and might like to speed up the hiring process, the reality is that teacher hiring ought to balance between the competing needs of finding an exceptional candidate for the current vacancy in the school while also ensuring that the candidate has the ability to perform well in another school. My experience is that teachers do not want to be "pigeonholed" into only fitting into a single school for their entire careers. A great many teachers want a chance to develop as professionals, and this includes being given the opportunity to teach in different grades and sometimes in different schools.

From a structural viewpoint, teacher hiring should be tied to a division's and a school's multiyear improvement plan. Teachers are hired into a division and subsequently assigned to schools, and therefore both divisional office and school administration necessarily have a vested interest in hiring the most effective teachers who can move the organization forward. A new teacher must do more than just fill the current vacancy. The teacher should bring the skills, experiences, and attitudes that help the whole system move in the direction it needs to go. Returning to a point made earlier in this chapter, the talents of "who" make the realization of the "what" of schooling possible.

Those charged at the divisional level with the responsibility of hiring teachers need to give much greater attention to how the various stages and processes of teacher screening and selection might be shared effectively between central office and school principals to ensure new hires are good for the whole school system. Arguably, it may be true, at times, that principals are in the best position to know "whom" they need to hire for their schools. But it is also important to recognize that many times that same teacher is also being hired into a division and can eventually move from one school to another. Therefore, while there is a pressing need to fill a specific job with a specific person, there is also a need to know if the teacher is a good fit for all of the schools in the division. Such an awareness of teacher fit on that grander scale might lie beyond the immediate horizon of any specific principal.

BREATHING SPACE

In an attempt to make the point that effective hiring is best left to those most possessing those skills, the sad but true demise of George O'Leary, the Notre Dame Fighting Irish football team coach who was hired—which means he applied and was interviewed for one of the most prestigious collegiate coaching jobs—and then resigned five days later will be used. On his résumé, O'Leary claimed to have a master's degree in education and to have played college football for three years. However, when officials at Notre Dame were tipped off that some of his claims did not match school records or his former teammates' recollections and checks into his background showed he had falsified it, O'Leary—faced with the prospect of being fired—chose to resign. In a statement released by Notre Dame University shortly after the details became public, O'Leary was quoted as saying, "Due to a selfish and thoughtless act many years ago, I have personally embarrassed Notre Dame, its alumni and fans. . . . Many years ago, as a young married father, I sought to pursue my dream as a football coach. . . . In seeking employment, I prepared a résumé that contained inaccuracies regarding my completion of course work for a Master's degree and also my level of participation in football at my Alma Mater. These misstatements were never stricken from my résumé or biographical sketch in later years."

The point is not about the morality or ethics of whether or not O'Leary purposefully lied, although obviously an interesting conversation point, but rather it is about highlighting the fact that, in the absence of diligent processes to verify the claims presented as fact in a résumé, an employer might not ever know the true background experience and qualifications of the adult he or she hires and leaves in charge of a classroom full of students.

It is not uncommon to read news reports that suggest a significant number, perhaps as many as one-third, of ten job seekers falsify their résumé and cover letter; they inflate their successes and diminish their shortcomings. In fact, during lean economic times, such as the one many teachers are now facing, when there is stiff competition to land a job, the percentage of people who commit résumé fraud increases. While it seems somewhat inconceivable to believe that an applicant might falsely claim to have a valid teaching certificate or to have graduated from an approved teacher preparation program when they did not, it is not improbable, especially in a tight job market, that what was actually a bachelor of science degree with a minor in chemistry may appear on a résumé as an honors bachelor of science degree with a major in chemistry. Without thorough background verification checks on educational achievement and employment history, it seems pointless to give credence to the "numerous summers spent working with inner-city youth at a community center" as listed in a résumé that may have in reality been two summers lifeguarding at the local wading pool in an affluent suburb. Just because something is eloquently written in a cover letter or appears on a résumé and sounds believable, the inconvenient truth is that many, including some readers of this book (and possibly its author in a youthful moment of indiscretion), have embellished their accomplishments. Placing blind trust without any verification of the facts borders on willful gullibility when hiring.

WHAT GETS COUNTED OUGHT TO MATTER

After the most capable hiring committee has been identified and given the necessary training, quantifying and qualifying the screening criteria, however it is done, is a critical first stage in selecting applicants who will be interviewed. It seems reasonable to presume the criteria that are assessed at this initial stage have been, if only loosely so, identified as being related to the kinds of knowledge, skills, dispositions, and experiences that might predict that one candidate demonstrates greater potential to be an effective teacher over another. Or at the very least, one might hope there is some evidence to suggest that they are reliable proxy measures that qualify a candidate's suitability to teach. Carefully assess the quality of evidence presented in the cover letters and résumés of the applicants against what you have determined is the "right stuff" required to be an effective teacher in your school or your division, and do the background checks on degrees, major accomplishments, and any other factors that could be exaggerated and might ultimately influence a hiring decision in favor of someone who is actually less qualified than another candidate.

INTERVIEWS

Properly conducted interviews provide a great deal of information about teacher thinking, intentions, and understanding. They allow two-way exchanges between assessor and candidate to occur and allow the former to probe more deeply in pursuing matters emerging in earlier parts of the evaluation process. There are very good reasons to hold interviews as part of the hiring process.

Interviews are, however, time consuming, difficult to score, and subject to interviewer bias. Such things as race, gender, ethnicity, height, and weight can skew an interviewer's assessment of a candidate's potential for on the job success. Candidates' verbal skills, because interviews rely on assessments of verbal fluency, oftentimes have a disproportionate influence on judgments made about their competency. Even though most people involved in the interview process are willing to admit that interviewing is an inherently flawed process that does not allow us to fully assess the actual potential of a candidate to get the work done, most people placed on hiring committees irrationally believe that they are the exception and that they can conduct an interview while suspending their biases. Yes, most interviewers, even in the absence of any demonstration of skills by the job candidate, through conversation alone will express great satisfaction that after this sit down conversation they have indeed identified the most excellent physics or physical education teacher from the pool.

The problem with all of this overconfidence and satisfaction on the part of the average evaluator is that the candidate's ability to create a good impression during an interview does not necessarily translate into effective teaching. According to Kenneth Peterson, the author of *Effective Teacher Hiring: A Guide to Getting the Best*, as common as interviews are in teacher hiring, the reality is that they are frequently used too early in the selection process and are overly focused on personal qualities that have nothing to do with what happens in the classroom. This is not to suggest that Peterson believes that interviews have no value or place in the screening and selection process. At later stages of the hiring process, interviews help clarify data from other sources, provide additional information about the applicant, and eliminate candidates who have trouble answering basic questions.

INTERVIEWING BLIND SPOTS

There are a few other specific human factors that interviewers should be aware of that anyone could fall victim to, which can influence our perceptions of someone. Figure 2.2 identifies how these factors can obscure evidence that should be assessed during the interview process.

The impact of these factors, however, can be lessened if interviewers are aware of them and how they shape their perceptions. Being aware of preferences and biases in hiring helps interviewers determine how much of their perception is being influenced by factors well beyond the scope of the interview. This awareness does not make them go away, and we should not expect that it would. Being aware, however, helps us to keep them in check.

FACTOR 1: LENIENCY OR STRINGENCY

- This is a tendency to rate candidates too harshly so that none of them meet your exacting criteria, or to be too easy on them so that all of them pass with flying colours.

FACTOR 2: HALO/HORN EFFECT

- This is a tendency to view attractive candidates more favourably than unattractive candidates. Taller candidates are seen as possessing greater capacity to lead as executives than are shorter candidates. Have you ever noticed how many CEOs are tall - over 6'? Candidates who have family or friends we approve of may rate higher than those who have family or friends we do not favour.

FACTOR 3: ERROR OF CENTRAL TENDENCY

- This is our tendency to give average marks to most of the candidates we interview. Whenever pollsters send out surveys, they have to be particularly careful not to ask questions that allow people to cluster their rankings toward the center or average of the response scale. They try their best to force a response to one side or the other of average because they know that very few people want to go out on a limb. Many people have the natural tendency to provide a lukewarm and noncommittal response, kind of like giving a "maybe."

FACTOR 4: STEREOTYPING

- In many cases, a male who applies for what is predominantly considered a female position – like being a Kindergarten teacher - has to be an amazing candidate to stand a chance or being hired. Similarly, a female may have to be assessed as being twice as good as some males to get offered a position in a male-dominated role; say like being Chief Superintendent of Schools which to this day is over-represented by males, especially given the predominance of females in the education system.

Figure 2.2.   Interviewing Blind Spots

BREATHING SPACE

Almost every employer requires three references from a prospective employee. When asked, however, "Why does almost everyone out there ask for three references?" the most common response that anyone wanting to volunteer an answer provides is, "Well, because that's what the guy before me did."

Repeatedly doing something without knowing why or if it truly produces results is not a hallmark of personnel leadership. It turns what is about to be research-based and professionally informed practice into the numb, heuristic, and baseless repetitive practice.

THE OBLIGATION TO CHECK THEM OUT

The reality of using three references in checking out a prospective hire is to ensure, as best as possible, that the information collected about an individual is from three independent sources. You should think about each reference check as a single data source about the specific person who wants to be hired. The information gathered can then be "triangulated" as external evidentiary points that will provide a more accurate and reliable "read" on where others external to the search process believe the applicant is located professionally and sometimes personally.

Information received through contacting the candidate's references regarding past work-related experiences and qualifications, in combination with the information gathered during the interview, will be invaluable in making a good hiring decision. Appropriate references are normally work-related and include, but may not be limited to, current and/or previous supervisors from comparable work contexts.

The purpose of the reference check is to verify the candidate's qualifications as they relate to the requirements of the vacant position. The reference check interview resembles the employment interview in that the questions asked are based on predetermined selection criteria. Following a specific format and asking previously determined interview questions that are aligned to the expectations of the job and the teaching and learning dynamic will help to ensure that the reference check covers the important areas related to the work of educating children. If all three data sources do not corroborate the information, you greatly increase the risk that the person is not well suited for the position. It does require contacting all three, even if you really are quite busy.

IT TAKES MONEY AND TIME TO HIRE WELL

In far too many school divisions, an organizational schism has been created whereby the human resource functions of creating or filling vacancies, either a new position or existing one, is done by people who are responsible for "hiring" without a clear connection to the "finance" folks who are responsible for budgeting for the initial and ongoing costs associated with recruiting, selecting, and retaining the personnel required for schooling. This separation implies that job creation and maintenance can take place without much consideration for the long-term financial commitments and constraints of the organization. It is an odd peculiarity when you think about it—the processes of hiring, professionally developing, and retaining great teachers cost money. Each year, as prices for goods and services escalate, those same very important functions will cost more money. Hiring needs to become a budgeted and accounted-for function of school leadership. Make no mistake about what is being proposed: School divisions and schools need to allocate enough money, time, and effort if they are truly committed to making hiring the most capable a priority and not an afterthought.

Personnel leadership needs to be conducted in the context of financial stewardship. Stewardship is about taking responsibility to wisely use the resources that are available—like money, time, and personnel. It is about being accountable to the public who has entrusted us with the resources. And each function—hiring well and financial responsibility—should inform the other, and neither one should drive the other. Developing a coherent strategic workforce plan, especially given that personnel costs account for anywhere from 75 to 85 percent of most schools' operating budgets, to align with the short- and long-term financial health of the organization is crucial. Those who lead and manage schools and divisions cannot neglect it.

SHORTCUTS LEAD TO PROBLEMATIC OUTCOMES

Although there might be a tendency to take shortcuts or circumvent the cumbersome rules of hiring, usually because school administrators do not think "the rules" apply to them, educators—all educators—have a legal and moral duty to treat people, even prospective employees, fairly. Federal and provincial/territorial legislation and divisional policies dictate hiring rules that need to be followed at all times. Superintendents, principals, and board members must conduct the screening and selection process by following the principles of natural justice and procedural fairness in order to address the inherent biases that are involved in the highly subjective act of assessing another human being.

Most institutions have a hiring system in place; most have had this system checked out by attorneys to make sure it is in compliance with every rule, regulation, and law that could govern it. Given the very private and sensitive nature of the information collected during the hiring process, the division or school should consult an attorney for guidance during the hiring system design phase to ensure that it meets the minimum legal standards. Prior to any system being implemented, it is prudent that it be thoroughly reviewed by a lawyer with expertise in labor practices to look specifically for an aggrieved candidate challenge to any parts of the process that may have the potential to violate her or his rights. Shortcuts in hiring and/or firing, whether chosen because they are convenient or have been passed down as tried and true, do not allow anyone to sidestep their legal and ethical obligations.

- **PRINCIPLE 3.6:** *Procedural shortcuts in hiring are tempting but are never worth it.*
- **PRACTICE 3.6:** *A measure of your leadership is found in your unwavering devotion to follow ethically fair and legally binding personnel management practices.*

THE COMPLEXITY OF TEACHING IS AMPLIFIED IN POORLY CONSTRUCTED TEACHER EVALUATION REGIMES

Each school day, millions of children arrive at their classroom doors hoping to find a dedicated, caring, and competent teacher ready to teach everyone who walks through the door. So do their parents and the public, in case anyone forgot to consider their hopes and aspirations for the education system. In order to increase the likelihood that this single expectation will be met day after day, the individuals who are recruited, prepared, and eventually hired need to be carefully chosen, and once given the opportunity to teach, it is imperative that they remain committed to improving themselves professionally. But they need guidance and help if they are to develop professionally in a manner that aligns with what is expected of them as teachers and what their teaching performance will be assessed against.

Professor Linda Darling-Hammond and her colleagues at Stanford University noted in their report *Creating a Comprehensive System for Evaluating and Supporting Effective Teaching* that the majority of existing teacher evaluation systems neither help teachers improve nor clearly distinguish between the teachers who are successful and those who are floundering in the classroom. Even though well-designed performance-based assessments have been found to measure aspects of teaching that are related to effectiveness as demonstrated by the research on effective teaching practice, teacher evaluation more often than not is regarded as a useless and time-consuming endeavor that rarely leads to improved professional practice. This disconnect should be concerning.

It is somewhat difficult to understand why some in leadership positions avoid admitting what folks within and outside of the education system readily acknowledge: The current system of hiring, supervising, professionally developing, and evaluating faculty and staff does not really work well because the parts are not regarded as belonging to a unified whole. It seems fair to suggest that currently almost all jurisdictions have a coherence and alignment problem. Each function of personnel leadership is treated distinctly and differently without much thought to developing them as part of a continuum. What we need to do is fairly simple. We need to commit to a continuum of professional development designed to support the ongoing advancement in the teaching and learning dynamic for the staff currently employed and open up a pathway that can be used to select the teachers we want to work with students. Figure 2.3 provides an illustrative example of what such a commitment might mean in practice.

The most elaborate teacher evaluation system is doomed to fail if teachers do not know what it takes to be considered effective and are not provided professional opportunities to develop their knowledge, skills, and dispositions from the first day on the job right through to the end of their career to become and remain effective. High-quality professional development must be not only available to every teacher but also more than an optional professional obligation. Throughout their careers, teachers need to be able to access targeted support that is specific to their career stage and addresses areas that have been identified for professional growth. This is a hallmark of professions—mandatory and ongoing professional development programs that are predicated on the assumption that professionals need to continuously develop the requisite competencies that separate the effective from the less than effective. Aimless self-directed professional development that is not mapped out against a framework of effective teaching is kind of like going to the casino, spinning the roulette wheel, and just hoping for a payoff. However, in the case of the casino, the players—teachers and students—lose most of the time.

SUMMARY

Rigorous hiring is built on the premise that, when in doubt, do not hire. Keep on looking. This is a much easier proposition to write than it is to enact. As the school year begins, you need to have someone ready to greet and teach the students. There is no value in me suggesting that you or your students are better served with a "teacher-less" classroom. You need to hire someone. So please do hire. But do not become so complacent that you have to settle

Develop agreement on a framework for effective teaching based on research. As necessary, make thoughtful modifications by taking into consideration any specific local contextual variables. This may require discussion and possibly rancorous debate, but research has demonstrated there are some shared characteristics that distinguish between effective and ineffective teaching practice.

Use the framework to focus attention on the teacher hiring criteria that are used to select the "most likely to succeed" in a classroom. Again take into consideration a jurisdiction's or school's specific needs for teachers.

Provide all teachers - newly hired and permanantly employed - with guidance on how they are doing in the classroom by providing understandable, regular and ongoing formative feedback. Feedback that is based on the same framework for effective teaching has been shared with them so they are aware of the areas that may be targeted for professional growth.

Insist on and provide each teacher with high-quality, targeted professional development - learning opportunities to improve professional practice - that match against the areas for growth identified through the formative assessment process.

Use the same framework for effective teaching to develop a process for summative assessment - an annual performance review - to let teachers know how they are doing over the academic year.

Professionally develop those who are responsible for supervising, coaching improvements in and assessing professional practice based on a framework for leading and managing a school's operations.

Figure 2.3.   Continuum for Professional Development

forever with what you chose out of a desperate need. Hiring someone, any-one, does not mean that you owe him or her anything more than the opportu-nity to be effective. Afford him or her the opportunity to be excellent and impress you.

With that said, it is obvious that there are some principals and superinten-dents who have settled for someone barely good enough and then became complacent with the fact that they have filled a hole and moved on. Some-time later they begin to wonder, sometimes out loud, who hired this weak teacher and offered her or him a permanent contract. The best-performing organizations, private or public, understand the concept of "quality" and its influence on success. They relentlessly and unapologetically seek the source of quality in formal schooling—namely outstanding teachers—as it is a noble and worthwhile quest for the closest thing that resembles the "Holy Grail" of effective schools.

The hiring decisions made by employers necessarily take place in a con-text of incomplete information. Employers cannot know the full productive capacities of job candidates before hiring them, and any hiring decision is inevitably an investment made under considerable uncertainty. Let go of any illusion you may hold that hiring can be made foolproof. It can be improved but will always remain imperfect.

There is little doubt that, though looking for a narrow conception or singular definition of what constitutes "good teaching" is about as practical as searching for unicorns, there are multiple and sometimes competing defi-nitions of "good teachers," and it seems fair to assume that potential employ-ers are invariably not interested in selecting and hiring "bad teachers." Thus, while operational definitions of a "good teacher" may vary across and within school divisions, in teacher selection processes, those responsible for teacher hiring should commit to the principles and practices. This will ensure that the hiring decisions they make reflect careful attention to the agreed-upon crite-ria assessed from the information gleaned from the application package, pre-employment interviews, reference checks, and any other evidence and that the assessments and weightings correlate with conceptions of what it means to be an effective teacher.

Hopefully this chapter has helped remind you of the "people-intensive" nature of schooling. The managerial and leadership moves involved with hiring personnel will benefit from a common grounding in the principles and practices that make for great personnel building. No discussion of personnel can happen without a serious discussion of finances. We have seen that school budgets reflect tremendous outlays for teachers, administrators, and staff. The next chapter delves into the intense financial commitment required to operate schools.

Chapter Three

Leadership Principles and Practices for Financial Management

Money is only a tool. It will take you wherever you wish, but it will not replace you as the driver.
—Ayn Rand, twentieth-century Russian-American novelist, philosopher, playwright, and screenwriter

This passage serves to highlight the sobering fact that some—including some school leaders—believe that all they need is greater access to money to address all the challenges that seemingly beleaguer schools. They do not seem to interrogate their assumption to discover whether or not the blind pursuit of more money will bring about greater educational opportunities for students to succeed by not questioning their own financial acumen. Money does not absolve leaders of having to make difficult resource allocation decisions.

BREATHING SPACE

It might seem like one of those rhetorical questions a professor of educational finance might ask his or her students to catch them off guard, but it is not intended to be one: "Would you let someone who does not have a proven and public track record of being capable to properly manage his or her own personal finances manage your money?" The reason to consider this question is the fact that principals commit quite a bit of energy and time to hone their leadership skills in various aspects of the teaching and learning dynamic but often fail to take their role as a steward of the public purse seriously. This is a shame because it is important that school leaders understand that it only takes a small amount of wrongdoing or even the perception of wrongdoing with

47

money—because of how it is viewed as both a means and an end and is an evocative entity—to weaken the public's trust in those responsible for leading schools. It is necessary, therefore, that those who make financial commitments with the public's money do so in ways that follow the generally acceptable guidelines and policies for stewarding the public purse and ensure that they and anyone else responsible for handling school money is given appropriate training.

- **PRINCIPLE 3.1:** *It's not your money—it belongs to the people.*
- **PRACTICE 3.1:** *School boards and schools do not own any of the financial resources they expend. The public, in the form of taxpayers, actually do. In democratic societies, the ways in which elected and appointed officials make financial decisions must be open, transparent, and worthy of the public's trust.*

THE POLITICS OF MONEY

Educational finance has a political basis wherein different interests push and pull in an attempt to obtain benefits and avoid undue burdens. Obviously, money matters. It is a resource that allows for the purchase of the requisite goods and services that will give students the best opportunities to learn. The financial structure of how schools are funded is also a reflection of the power structure within the educational system. It therefore makes some sense to briefly explore the interrelated power structures and political bases for formal education.

While local governments—in the form of local school boards—may have limits on their abilities to generate revenues, they are afforded a fair amount of discretion to make decisions with respect to the expenses in the form of the levels of educational programs and services that are offered in the local school(s). This is why the school board's budgetary deliberations—the annual meetings—are, or least should be, the most highly attended meetings by parties interested in quality education. This overarching political and financial structure continues to exist by and large today, and it is an important sociohistorical legacy that permeates many of the decisions that affect how schools are operated, as decisions concerning revenues and expenditures are intertwined with issues of power related to determining what constitutes the common good at the school and community levels.

Based on anticipated revenues, school boards make decisions about how much they can spend and develop budgets that are designed to appropriately take into consideration local expectations of what schools need to offer. By way of example, they may ask such questions as, Should a school have a teacher librarian or a library technician? Or, based on the monies we have, do we want a full- or part-time vice principal or a teaching principal or a principal who does not teach? In addition, they may have to decide what technology or furnishings they want to purchase to respond to calls to be twenty-first-century schools. In some cases, boards distribute funding to hire a certain number of teachers to staff a school depending on the number of students and, in some cases, make changes to the teacher-to-pupil ratio to accommodate students who might struggle to succeed because of various factors or needs that make learning in large classes difficult. Boards may be allowed to decide which schools should stay open and which should close and how many custodians, secretaries, and educational assistants each school will get. School boards play a significant role in how money is disbursed.

The divisional budget is the most important tool used by school boards to ensure its financial commitments are being responsibly discharged. School divisions prepare budgets on a regular basis and use them as both a financial planning tool and as a control mechanism. Approval and monitoring of the division's as well as the school budgets is one of the most critical roles of the elected trustees. When a school board approves the financial statements presented at a board meeting or a local school council approves the school budget presented at its meeting, it means that they—the people chosen to represent and safeguard the intentions of the public—understand and agree with the information contained in the budgetary reports. Vigilance over the financial health of a limited public purse is a vital element of local school governance and one that all school officers, elected and appointed, ought to take seriously. School officers—superintendents, secretary-treasurers, and principals—are employees who have been delegated authority to make some financial decisions on how best to spend the public's money.

In the book *Good to Great*, Jim Collins argues that budgeting needs to be considered as a discipline that helps those responsible for the organization decide which programs and services should be funded, either partially or fully, and which should not be funded at all. In the context of developing a budget for a division or a school, the budget process is not really just about figuring out how much a program or an activity gets. It is also fundamentally about determining the activities that best support the division's or school's mission and priorities and thus should be bolstered through funding or be eliminated in part or entirely. Budgeting, at least budgeting exceptionally well, requires remarkable focus, skill, and courage.

Channeling finite financial resources into the areas that are a priority for a local school, especially if this is an area in which the school might be able to do exceptionally well, can yield tremendous benefits for students. For example, committing abundant financial resources to bilingual education programs where parents are motivated to support their children's fluency in two languages and in communities that provide students with opportunities to use both the languages outside of the classroom makes a lot of sense.

However, such commitments are oftentimes going to meet with some political pushback. Few educational leaders have the stomach to take a position that not everything that schools are expected to do ought to be done. However, the end result of not prioritizing some programs and initiatives over others is that few are actually provided with the appropriate level of funding that would maximize the effects for students.

Importantly, school trustees are locally elected officials who are responsible and answerable not to some anonymous electorate but instead to their neighbors, whom they see at church, the coffee shop, or an arena on a regular basis and who trust them, albeit at times uncomfortably so, to spend their money. Elected trustees should never shy away from asking superintendents where the money was spent. In fact, not asking is a dereliction of one of their most important public duties.

It is suggested from time to time that school boards should be eliminated because they represent antiquated conservative notions of government of unified homogeneous communities that no longer exist today. Advocates for maintaining them contend that school boards are grassroots democracy in action. In reality, school boards and their trustees are caught in a political squeeze between provincial departments of education who want greater centralized uniformity and school-based parent groups who are fighting for even more localized decision-making powers. It is hard to imagine a less-valued public leadership position today than that of a school trustee.

In turn, trustees work with the central administrative staff—the superintendent and secretary-treasurer—to develop a budget for the schools. In some cases but not all, principals receive a budget for the school from the school board. While some monies might be raised at the local level to support extracurricular programs or noncore educational services and programs, the majority of the budget is set. Principals might get to make decisions or be consulted about the distribution of teachers and class sizes or about school maintenance and repairs within a school's budget. Sometimes they decide how to allocate educational assistants and whether their school can have staff such as a teacher, librarian, music teacher, or department heads that receive additional release time. Depending on the size of the school, principals may also allocate funding to different academic departments. From time to time principals may make decisions on school fees and, with the school council, may decide where fund-raised money will be spent.

Principals can thus be described as lowercase "p" politicians. As much as they hate to admit it, they represent some of the power and political structure of the school system because they oftentimes get to decide how some of the finite financial resources are distributed within schools and because they interact with the public on a daily basis. They might be involved in the decisions about what gets funded and sometimes have to fight to retain what is not going to get funded. In essence, in a very tangible way, they operate as power brokers in the system, cutting deals to make things work for students, teachers, parents, and the school community. They in fact have a fair amount of power within the system at the local level. As much as principals may cringe at the suggestion, it is impossible to ignore how they are coupled to the structure, finance, and power of the school system.

Taking this principle seriously creates unique challenges for the stewardship of public funds. One challenge that school leaders face related to communicating the bases of the contestable financial decisions that must be made in an era of increased expectations for financial transparency and accountability is around this issue of proper justification of expended funds. This is a result of the fact that school leaders typically lack a sufficiently sophisticated level of financial literacy to effectively communicate the financial principles that structured their decision-making process. And it is compounded by the fact that it is hard for all of the stakeholders in a school to come to a consensus about financial priorities once they have been communicated in a transparent manner. Despite the fact that financial decision making is more complex today than ever before, there are still no requirements that those educational leaders must be financially literate. This is true even though a lack of financial knowledge will inevitably result in ill-informed decisions being made. And how many school leaders with or without financial literacy can articulate in language that is not veiled in jargon how and why certain decisions were made?

There is a saying that is arguably attributed to the legend of the Pied Piper of Hamelin that goes something like this: "He who pays the piper calls the tune." For many people, not just school leaders, this saying manifests as a form of paralysis in which they believe that only those who have the authority to make money decisions have the decisive position of power in the organization. And unfortunately, this belief makes them care less about understanding the complexities of budgeting.

But the individuals in school leadership positions need to commit and spend time trying to understand how the money is being spent and the impact of the spending on achieving the intended outcomes of the expenditures in order to create realistic and appropriate budgets. There are no magic elixirs or mystical incantations that exist to resolve the impediments associated with drawing on finite financial resources to fund infinite expectations of what schools can achieve. What is needed is a level of financial awareness that allows school leaders to examine whether or not adequate financial, human, and space resources have been allocated and whether or not these are sustainable in the future to support a school's particular priorities.

- **PRINCIPLE 3.2:** *Leading a school requires financial literacy.*

- **PRACTICE 3.2:** *The ability to make informed judgments and to make effective decisions regarding the use and management of money has to be learned in theory and in practice.*

LEARNING HOW TO DISCUSS THE UNDISCUSSABLE

As was the case then and in the centuries prior, more contemporary ideas of what constitutes financial leadership require the development of management knowledge and skill, which has three constitutive elements to it:

- financial acumen,
- understanding resource acquisition, and
- understanding resource allocation.

Figure 3.1 provides an illustrative example of the interconnectedness of the three elements of financial leadership.

In order to develop what can be termed *financial literacy*, time, energy, and effort need to be committed by school leaders and their employers. First, while it is fundamentally important to choose educators who can serve educational leaders, it is also critical that central office administrators look for talented and committed educators who are willing to become competent

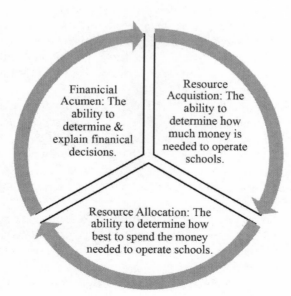

Figure 3.1.   Financial Leadership Sectors

financial leaders in their school communities. Financial leadership is not considered to be glorious work in education, but it is important. Much like learning or striving to be a "good" teacher requires work and focus, the notion of someone being able to provide financial leadership is a reasonable expectation to hold for those who choose to become school leaders.

Having people understand and appreciate the decisions about how best to make use of scant and ever-shrinking financial resources available to fund schooling is not as meaningful in the context of school operations unless the stakeholders of schooling—teachers, parents, students, and the public at large—believe the decision makers truly understand the core financial principles of their decisions. Effectively articulating why some initiatives and programs were funded while others were not is an opportunity to build confidence in the public that those responsible for making important financial decisions are knowledgeable and competent financial stewards of public funds and that they possess an adequate degree of knowledge of financial principles, budgetary approaches, and models. It does not guarantee that the public will understand or agree with the decisions that must be made by those responsible for leading schools. It should, however, illustrate that those responsible for making the decisions should understand the basics of public sector finance in the context of education.

It is therefore imperative that school leaders—principals, superintendents, and board officers—remember that the public office they hold is in fact a very real form of public trust. The authority and opportunities that derive from holding a formal position of leadership in a school should be used with as much care and stewardship as is owed the public who have entrusted you to hold the office and literally spend their money. In terms of school and division finances it is indeed the public's money, and it ought to be used for the public's benefit and not for the purposes of furthering any individual ideology, philosophy, or vision.

At this point, it seems prudent to introduce a concept that will be more fully examined in the next chapter, namely relational trust in schools. In the face of increasing numbers of public scandals that involve the misuse or misappropriation of other people's money, it seems important to consider the question: What can school leaders do to restore the public's trust in others with their money? It means that you conduct yourself at all times in ways that will honor the trust people place in you and more broadly in those who hold leadership roles in the education system to make decisions.

Most people are willing to take a chance and give you the benefit of the doubt even if they do not personally know you. In simple terms: They are willing to extend a certain amount of trust to you. After that, though, you need to start earning it. It is your job to provide them with the kind of evidence that reassures them their initial trust was well vested and ought to be extended.

Learning how to manage money is an acquired skill, and for many people that learning comes with some measure of trial and error. Sometimes and unfortunately, the error can be bankrupting, literally, and, depending on what kind of decisions were made that led to the financial collapse, potentially morally as well. The fact that some people are forced to declare personal bankruptcy should not, however, be used as an excuse to allow schools to accidentally and repeatedly overspend the hard-earned money that the public has entrusted to school leaders.

Many people learn the lessons of maintaining financial solvency quickly and easily, while others learn it neither quickly nor easily. In that latter group, far too many borrow too much money to pay for a lifestyle they have seen on reality television but one they cannot really afford. As they live off what appears, at least at first blush in this day and age, to be "cheap credit," they do so without much thought about the inevitable fact that the cost of servicing the debt they incurred, which supports a lifestyle they have grown accustomed to and cannot live without, increases exponentially as interest rates rise. They have succumbed to a spending addiction, all the while blind to the fact that their expectations of what constitutes living a good life may ultimately cripple them financially. To a disturbingly large extent, the broke are relying on credit cards and lines of credit to make it until their next payday.

It would be disingenuous to suggest that many of these individuals do not learn and recover. Some but not all do—learn that is. If the economic roller-coaster of the early twenty-first century has taught us anything, however, it is that many people do not learn the hard financial lessons of life and that, once they financially "get their heads above water," they begin to spend and borrow again. It is as if living off borrowed money has become an addiction of the times.

Recognizing the truth inherent in such a proposition, why then would we believe that these same folks would behave any differently if given access to the public purse? By opportunistically rephrasing a quote attributed to Aristotle, an attempt is made to emphasize a point in case it has not been clear: We are what we repeatedly do, like overspending. Weak financial steward-ship is a learned habit of being. It is not a random act of a single bad budget cycle repeating itself over and over again but rather a habit of the financially illiterate.

Attend any school board budget meeting, and you will witness an example of the abundant evidence that suggests that the communication of "how" financial decisions are made, especially the more controversial ones, in schools and/or systems are often handled poorly. Conduct a Google search, and you can see immortalized episodes of school board budget meetings gone wild if you do not believe me. Let's face one of those inconvenient truths: A whole lot of folks are very uncomfortable discussing finances, be they personally or professionally related, and they tend to fumble their way through them. We never really learn how to discuss money matters, and this is especially true with discussing them at work. We just assume that people will mysteriously figure out how to converse about such matters as: How much is a person's teaching work actually worth? What is the limit to funding a specific student activity? How many computers do we really need in a school? It seems as if most educators would rather not keep the budget discussion going constantly in parallel to the program and idea discussions. It is as if they want to avoid placing a dollar value on anything they offer in terms of programs and services, and so they do not.

In the face of claims that business and school are antithetical concepts, is the reality that every moment in a school day can be framed from a business or financial outlay perspective. From the moment you enter a school—a school whose budget must be balanced and a school in which the public hands over their money with the expectation that each student will receive an appropriate education that meets her or his unique learning needs, all the while not increasing their tax burden—there are operational aspects related to the school that ought to be businesslike. Clearly, not every action you will undertake as an educational leader has a business component to it that must be managed. Nor should they be operated as businesses to the detriment of the learning environment or well-being of students and staff. In fact, at a well-run school, well-managed financial decisions will allow most people to not think so much about finances but more about education. Educating children is not akin to the mass production of precise widgets. Education systems, however, do have real costs associated with running them, and possessing the financial wherewithal to lead them is vitally important.

BREATHING SPACE

The story did not make the front page of the mainstream media in Liberty City, but it did garner some attention in a smaller independent news outlet and a few community blog posts. The reports suggested that the Liberty City Regional School District owed North American Steel Products roughly $2.1 million.

In the official minutes from the school district's June board meeting, it was noted that the school board had reached an out-of-court settlement with North American Steel Products. The details in the minutes were vague but indicated there had been a lengthy legal battle over the "true" assessed value of two of North American Steel Products' facilities located within Liberty City. North American Steel had demonstrated that an overzealous city tax assessor, who happened to be the brother-in-law of one of the school district's board members, had improperly assessed the North American Steel

Products locations as "operational" rather than as "dark facilities"—in essence they were just large storage yards for raw steel. The improper assessment had resulted in an overcharge of the industrial school taxes.

The school district's lawyers had argued it was not responsible for the error, had expended the monies on much-needed school improvements, and could not repay the monies. However, fearing a lengthy and public court battle that might expose a lack of financial oversight by the board, the legal team recommended that Liberty City Regional School District settle the matter. However, as the June minutes also showed, in order to do so, the school district was required to reduce the educational programs and services it offered, initiate staff layoffs, and seek permission to retroactively increase the residential property tax mill rate.

- **PRINCIPLE 3.3:** *Schools are capital-intensive operations that require enormous and ongoing financial commitments.*
- **PRACTICE 3.3:** *Principals need to be responsible stewards of the limited public funds that are available to pay for schooling and not treat the budget like a limitless line of credit.*

FINANCING THE COMMON GOOD

In some regards, a lot of the sociohistorical contextual challenges have changed since the contemporary public school system in North America was set up. It is hard but not impossible to still find a one-room schoolhouse. It is becoming increasingly rare to find anyone but a university-educated adult with a level of specialized knowledge in the role of teacher. It is equally difficult to find anyone in a school leadership role who argues against the premise that one of the fundamental goals of education is to prepare young people for the "real world," even if finding agreement on what constitutes the real world of schools is ontologically debatable.

Other things have not changed much. The idealism of a formal education remains intact. Teaching is still considered more like an art than a science, and the challenges that present themselves with trying to have the correct mix of direct instruction and discovery learning that will prepare an increasingly diverse school community to continue to exercise both the mind as well as the heart have endured.

It is hard to argue, however, with the fact that in the past two hundred years formal education has become increasingly connected and intertwined with business operations, even though there exists a chorus of educational puritans who believe there must be a complete dissociation between the principles of education and business. These folks recoil at the suggestion that the terms "school" and "business" could ever be uttered in the same breath, and they believe that their role is to guard against any comingling between the ideals of education and the financial principles of business. By now they have probably given up reading this book.

It seems to be taken for granted in many quarters these days that, when it comes to funding public schools, formal education should not really be regarded as a cost but rather as an investment in human capital. It seems as if such sentiments have existed for at least a few centuries. There is nothing fundamentally wrong with accepting this idealized principle. Society should invest in developing the capabilities of young people to do a great many things that may ultimately improve quality of life as we collectively enjoy it.

However, much has changed in society since the formation of the modern public education system, which, for North America, was created to align with somewhat nationalistic, if not parochial, notions of the "common good" and financed in ways to fulfill a nineteenth-century understanding of what it meant to commit to that promise. Drawing on early- to mid-twentieth-century notions of the common good, formal education was regarded as one of society's great mass social institutions that could contribute to a vision of the good life for Canadians and Americans.

This commitment to fund public education was influenced by the work of John Locke, a seventeenth-century British philosopher who argued that, when people enter a society, they give up some liberties to gain the protection of a larger set of liberties and rights as part of a social contract. A society knitted together by the "common good," Locke proposed, guarantees rights that would not have existed in a presocial setting. Public education was regarded as the primary social instrument of the notion of the common good, and in fact such a strong belief in their power to make real the notion of the common good led in many practical ways to the establishment and continuance of the various regulations that govern the public school system. Such things as compulsory attendance, age-graded classrooms, the regulation of patriotic school activities, and the common curriculum are all largely premised on this rationale.

The establishment of public schools and the financing of them from a tax base that everyone paid into was justified in terms of benefits to the public of having an educated civil society. It was not justified in terms of such private advantages as greater knowledge, higher social standing, or greater earning potential but because publicly funded schools would inevitably contribute to the "common good" by imparting the kinds of values and normalized behaviors that would benefit the entire society. The question of what is the "common good" and how schools can help achieve it has been a source of debate in Canada and the United States, two countries that, perhaps surprisingly, lack national education systems. While different, each nation boasts a predominantly decentralized educational legal framework that assigns an aspirational commitment to use formal education as means to develop something referred to as the "common good" of building a nation to the various provinces', territories', or states' legislatures. And in recent years, during a period of increased economic pressure to prepare global citizens, thoughtful discussions about what constitutes the common good have become scarce.

BORDERS AND DISSIMILAR FUNDING

The United States of America

Similar to the case in Canada, the U.S. Constitution primarily anchors the responsibility for the provision of kindergarten through grade 12 education with the fifty states. The fifty states in turn over time have established tens of thousands of school districts and hundreds of thousands of schools, all for the purpose of delivering K–12 education to students at the local level.

Beginning around the mid-1960s, the U.S. federal government began to make money available to fund public education through some specific federal legislative acts, such as the Elementary and Secondary Education Act (ESEA), the precursor to the much-vilified No Child Left Behind Act. As a result, on average, the federal government currently provides about 10 percent of the funds required to operate public education. The money is tied to federal legislation that intended to increase educational access, opportunity, and quality for students across the United States.

Of the remaining 90 percent required to run public schools, nearly half of the money is raised through local taxation. The other 45 percent comes from the state. This funding approach has resulted in some very large differences in the monies available to operate schools in more affluent communities in comparison to those that have higher levels of poverty. As a result, the disparities that exist in per-pupil funding levels are often greater within states than they are across the fifty state lines. It is important to note, though, that debates have existed for decades in the United States and also in Canada on whether or not more money results in better student achievement.

The U.S. federal and state governments provide very little capital funding for school facilities, and therefore the financial burdens associated with new construction and capital improvements rest mostly on the shoulders of local school districts. Far too often, districts have no choice but to draw on operational budgets—the same budgets that pay for salaries, instructional materials, and general programming—to fix a leaky roof. School districts use bonds to borrow money from future years' budgets to pay for more expensive capital projects like major heating, cooling, and ventilation improvements. School districts cannot, however, just issue bonds whenever they need. In order to issue a bond, a school district must gain approval from the local electorate. If they are fortunate to get their approval, the district sells the bonds and pays them back with interest by raising local school taxes in future years.

Canada

The early funding mechanisms in Canadian provinces in the post-1867 constitutional era were designed to support the establishment and operations of small local school divisions that reflected the hopes and aspirations of what might be best described as tightly knit and homogeneous local communities. Originally signed in 1867 and then repatriated in 1982, the Constitution of Canada gives exclusive power to make laws in relation to education to the provincial legislatures. And in turn, provincial and territorial governments have historically shared responsibility for funding schools with local municipalities and school boards.

As part of the delegation of responsibility to the provinces to establish schools in a newly created Canada, the provinces granted local governments, in the form of elected school boards, the authority to collect substantial portions of education funding from the local property tax base. Over time, however, an analysis of the educational funding in Canadian provinces reveals a trend away from primarily local taxation to fund schools toward joint provincial-local and in many cases full provincial funding.

Across Canada's provincial and territory boundaries, governments have increasingly started to impose restrictions on how much money can be generated from local tax bases and how these monies can be spent. Governments have largely eliminated the direct collection of local taxes to exclusively fund local school board programs and initiatives in favor of a scheme of distributing locally raised taxes provincially. All of Canada's provincial or territorial governments and locally elected school boards can in general be characterized as comanaging the financial resources of the education system. Each province or territory establishes the amount of grant funding for public education annually and uses a funding formula to allocate these funds to the local school boards or independent schools. Provincial and territorial regulations, revised yearly, provide the grant structure that sets the level of funding for each school board based on factors such as the number of students, the number of students with special needs, targeted populations who need additional support, specialized programs that are beyond core programming, and school locations. School boards, in turn, manage and allocate their provincial allotment based on local spending priorities. In addition, each province generally provides capital costs and funding for most special programs through supplemental government funds and grants.

THE COMMON IRK OF TAXATION

Generating the money necessary to educate millions of school-aged children in North America is a relatively straightforward endeavor. Taxation, and this has been the case for well over a century, is the principle mechanism for collecting the revenues necessary to operate public schools. That said, however, any straightforward clarity in understanding the complexity of a system of convoluted revenue streams that underwrites public education is impossible in a single chapter. With such an admission, it is still important for school leaders to have some basic knowledge of how the school taxation mechanisms are employed in North America.

In its most simple form, property tax is levied on the value of the property, not the owner's equity. If, for example, you live in a home worth $300,000, the school taxes are levied on the assessed value. It does not matter if you own it or still owe money on it when it comes to taxation. Unlike other forms of taxation, school-based property tax is a tax on an asset rather than a financial flow. Municipalities have, for centuries, relied on this form of taxation to pay for municipal services and programs. So, too, for well over a century, have schools.

The amount of tax payable per dollar of the assessed value of a property is calculated based on the assessed value of the property multiplied by the established mill rate and divided by one thousand. The mill rate is based on "mills": as each mill is one-thousandth of a currency unit, one mill is equivalent to one-tenth of a cent, or $0.001. As a property may be subject to tax by a number of different authorities, mill rates are set by each taxing authority (school boards and/or municipalities) so as to meet the revenue projections in their budgets. For a given jurisdiction, mill rates may depend on the classification of property, whether it is residential, commercial, industrial, agricultural, and so on.

Figure 3.2 offers an example of using a hypothetical mill rate to calculate the dollar amount of school taxes based on residential property valuation. In theory, consider a property with an assessed value of $300,000 that is located in a school division with a mill rate of 10. The school taxes levied would therefore be a product of $300,000, multiplied by 10, divided by 1,000, which would result in $3,000 of school taxes owed by the property owner annually.

As property values increased in the past number of decades in many North American real estate markets, so did the revenues school divisions garnered in the form of property taxes without the need to actually raise the mill rate. The rise of home values in Canada during the closing of the twentieth century and into the very early part of the following decade provided an influx of school taxes to school divisions without the requirement to raise the mill rate, even though many have still done so. The turbulence associated

Portioned assessment of property/home valuation	Multiply	School Division Mill Rate (for this example set at 10 Mills)	Divided by 1000	Equals	School division taxes
$300,000	*X*	*10*	*÷ 1000*	*=*	*$3000 payable in school taxes*

Figure 3.2.   Overview of Mill Rate Calculation

with the mid-2000s financial crash, largely attributable to a housing market buoyed by bad mortgage loans, changed that certainty. Any significant correction to the real estate market, as in a bursting of the bubble, would cause significant budget contractions as home values plummet and the school taxes collected based on their values concomitantly fall.

Beyond monies raised locally, typically in the form of school or property taxes, income, consumption, and wealth taxes and federal transfer payments are used to help fund the provision of educational services and programs. While the particular details of each jurisdiction's approach to generating revenues can and do vary, it is safe to say that the goal of the funding system is to collect sufficient revenues that provide a politically justifiable level of financial resources to sustain the operation of the K–12 system by applying formulae to ensure a relatively equitable taxation system across the breadth of each province, territory, and state and within each local school jurisdiction.

The majority of school finance models currently in use, especially at the local level, are not typically designed to support uniformly high levels of student achievement, and this is particularly acute in a period of schools welcoming an increasingly diverse school population. The funding formulae still in place today by and large reflect an era when not all children were expected to succeed at school or in life. It was not that long ago that society commonly accepted that anywhere from 30 to 40 percent of school children would not graduate from high school. Nowadays anything less than a 99 percent graduation rate is considered to be failing. Such high expectations can be contrasted with the fact that most of the funding arrangements that exist today are remnants of a system that was designed to not allow all to graduate. For some inexplicable reason, we cling to a funding scheme, perhaps out of fear, designed for a much lower "success" rate, at least in terms of graduation, even though our expectations for inclusion and "education for all" were never part of the design of the archaic funding regime. Somehow we expect to do more and better without seriously rethinking how we need to pay for schooling.

How then should society determine how much it is willing to spend on education? Theoretically the process is not all that dissimilar to deciding how much you will spend on a glass of water. Before you jump to answer this question, consider the following two possibilities: What are you willing to pay for an ice-cold, pure glass of water if you are stuck:

• in the desert on a hot day?

OR

• in the rain on a cold day?

There are, of course, other fictitious, sensational scenarios that can be conjured up, but most likely you get the point. The value of the worth of that glass of water is, in part, determined by how vitally it is needed by the purchaser.

Running schools—and improving their operations—cannot take place without the proper resources, and acquiring the necessary resources in the form of goods and/or services requires money—in many cases a substantial amount of money. Very few in the education system seem to be willing to admit that there might not actually be enough money available through the public purse to fund all of the aspirational goals that society has for schooling. Everyone wants so much out of the system, and it is hard to imagine a time when these expectations will completely disappear. The truth is, though, that there may never be enough money available to fund all of the priorities. And in some cases relatively small improvements can be extremely expensive.

Clear evidence of how much money should be collected and spent, what programs and initiatives must be funded, and which are the ones best positioned to support schoolwide student achievement remains elusive. If increases in financial resources had the clear and consistent effect of improving student outcomes, budgeting would be straightforward. However, it does not, and it is not.

In an era of increased public scrutiny of how the taxpayers' monies are spent and aggressive calls for educational reforms, school divisions are being pressured to work within the existing financial constraints to produce budgets that support a greater number of demands, including the needs of all students. In essence, school personnel are asked to do more for students without any additional financial resources. In the pall of very limited means of generating revenues, much of the work of school leaders is on how best to make use of the limited financial resources available.

• **PRINCIPLE 3.4:** *Allocating finite resources (money) is an inherently imperfect endeavor.*

- **PRACTICE 3.4:** *Schools as socially constructed organizations provide a power base for individuals, and this is nowhere more evident than in the decisions related to the allocation of scarce financial resources.*

FACING HARSH REALITIES

Many people think budgets are only algorithms—step-by-step procedures of adding, subtracting, multiplying, and dividing numbers—and nothing more. What gets lost in such a simplistic understanding is the fact that budgets are very tangible commitments to what organizations value. School budgets are no different, and financial decisions are debated, sometimes heatedly, because the budget attempts to find common ground and commitment to many and oftentimes competing values. Which values matter most, particularly in dollars and cents, will always be contested.

It is common for school districts and schools to have a mission statement that expresses the school community's collective hopes and dreams for its children. As much as they are maligned as being overly idealistic, mission statements serve a useful purpose when they signal to those who work within the system—students, parents, teachers, and community partners—and those who live their lives outside the system—the general public—what the school values. A mission statement is a public acknowledgment of an organization's direction and ought to be instructive in the establishment of priorities that will move the school closer to fulfilling its goals. In a budgeting context, understanding what a school or district aspires to be offers to the public some valuable insight into the decision-making process about what services and programs should be funded and which should not.

BREATHING SPACE

First-century Roman philosopher and playwright Seneca the Younger observed: "If a man knows not what harbor he seeks, any wind is the right wind." In simple terms, if a school community does not keep its agreed-upon aspirations—its mission—in focus during its budgeting deliberations and decision making, then any arbitrary approach to allocating money is as good as any other. "Idiosyncrasy rules" would be the appropriate mantra. Without a clear sense of what the priorities are and what the school hopes to be and provide for students, parents, the local community, and the public at large, every initiative is equally important and deserving of funding. Everything gets a sprinkling of money, and therefore bits and pieces of various initiatives get some financial support, but nothing gets fully funded or accomplished.

It is the quackery of such sloganism as: "Throw everything at the wall and something will certainly stick." If you honestly take the time to visualize that profane metaphoric reference, you will see a whole lot of time, energy, commitment, and money that is not your own that is left lying in a pile of refuse at the foot of the wall from the ideas that did not stick, while some are left hanging by a few tattered threads. It seems patently unfair to do this to other people—their time, energy, and commitment can so easily be wasted on someone's hare-brained ideas.

STRETCHING LIMITED RESOURCES

In the end, many of the people responsible for funding schools recognize that there will never be enough money to appropriately meet the learning and developmental needs of all students. Each and every year, the expectations of what schools are to provide students academically, socially, emotionally, and psychologically grow well beyond the limited funding increases that flow to them, but still very few are willing to suggest there is a need for a radical overhaul to change the funding mechanism. It is a discomforting position to find ourselves in, at least as educators. Very few are fully satisfied with maintaining the status quo of the funding arrangements, yet the complexity of committing to a complete overhaul paralyzes everyone from taking a risk to try out new funding arrangements. This continues to leave us with an intractable problem.

Fear of the unknown is an extremely powerful force. Consequently, what exists today are funding formulae so incongruent and so complex that they are difficult to understand and even more impervious to analyze with respect to the effects of the expenditures on student achievement measures. We trudge along begrudging the fact that there is not enough "money in the system," yet too afraid to audaciously try to rebuild the system to reflect the twenty-first century rather than the nineteenth.

There are a wide range of estimates for what researchers and educators believe a "high-quality education" actually costs. Conversations about how much a quality education costs become muddled by issues such as

- the assortment of ill-defined ideas of what makes for successful class-rooms and schools,
- poorly conceived estimates of the cost functions in the form of estimates of inputs (money) and outputs (the goals of a system educating massive numbers of children).
- arguments over what constitutes evidence of success in education (for example, increasing graduation rates, literacy rates, self-esteem indexes, or decreasing teen pregnancy rates), and

- a lack of consensus on whose judgment matters most; namely do superintendents, principals, teachers, parents, or students get to decide what constitutes a high-quality education?

In light of this litany of woes it is perhaps not surprising that those committed to education do not eagerly entertain difficult discussions about what an education ought to cost.

It has been reported in a source no less credible than Wikipedia that the *Oxford English Dictionary* credits the June 20, 1959, edition of the *New York Times* as containing the first recorded print use of the idiomatic phrase, "it's time to acknowledge the elephant in the room." It is purported that the phrase was drawn from the following statement:

> Financing schools has become a problem equal to having an elephant in the living room. It's so big you just can't ignore it.

The imagery of the phrase suggests that there are some issues so large, so obvious, and so noticeable that the fact that no one is discussing their presence is hard to comprehend. Still, they are not discussed. The irony of the plausible origin of the phrase should also not be lost as you read this chapter.

Not only is there an elephant in the room in the form of the school finance squeeze, but there are in fact several lumbering around, waiting for school leaders to notice their enormity and capacity for influencing, well, everything within the school. Luckily, these elephants are sitting, so to speak, in the living room of a chapter that is all about school finance. With respect to some of the assumptions that influence funding decisions, they are rarely discussed publicly. That said, any attempt to offer more would leave readers wondering if they were stuck in the midst of an episode of *Babar*.

For simplicity's sake, the four elephants, representing the taken-for-granted assumptions that are rarely deliberated in the sobriety of public discourse, can be initially presented embedded in one fundamental question that is both philosophically complex and also operationally problematic. However difficult, it is a question that ought to be considered by those responsible for the financial operations and health of schools and school divisions: Is the quality of the education that we want to fund based on a principle of (1) adequacy, (2) equality, (3) equity, or (4) appropriateness of educational opportunities?

Even though it is tempting to say all of the above, the reality is that achieving any one of these outcomes singularly is a monumental challenge. How school leaders respond to this question will provide tremendous insight into how they believe the limited resources available to schools and divisions should best be distributed to achieve the aims of schooling.

ILLUSTRATING THE TENSIONS

A visual model is simply an illustration of an abstract concept: Text and lines are intended to partially illustrate a story. Such is the case in figure 3.3. It is limited in scope, as each of the four concepts is inextricably complex. It is, however, offered as a representation of the intricacy of determining the cost of an education.

Before providing a few examples to illustrate the tensions that exist among these concepts, it is worth noting that much of education funding is tied to school enrollment numbers. The vast majority of the revenues that divisions and schools receive are based on a student count (also called student enrollment) at a given time, and this "number" of students generates the

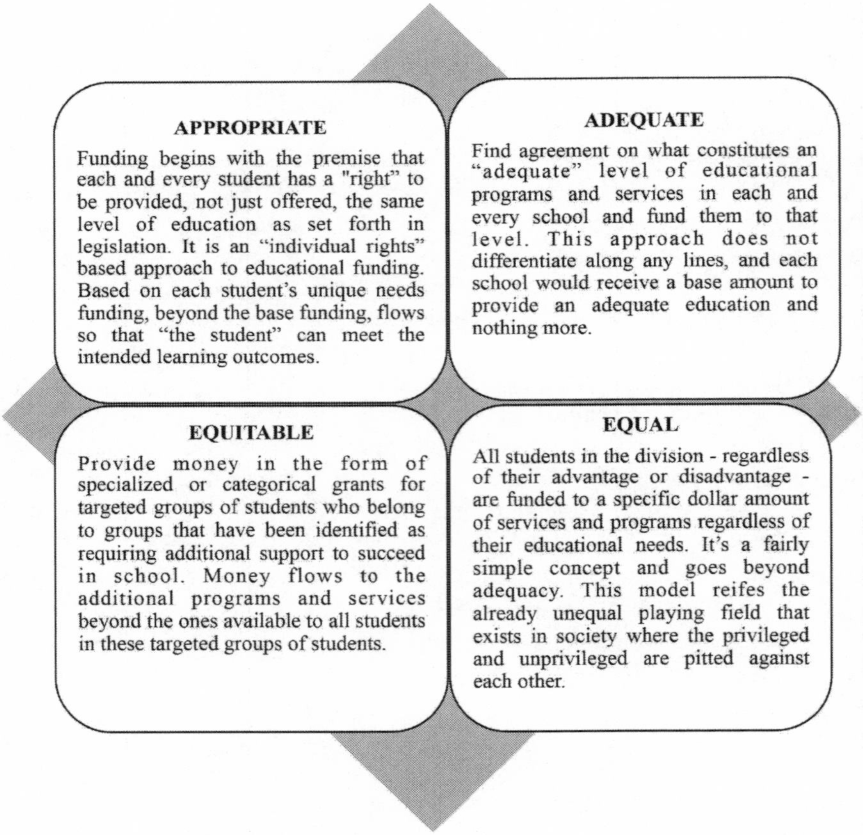

APPROPRIATE

Funding begins with the premise that each and every student has a "right" to be provided, not just offered, the same level of education as set forth in legislation. It is an "individual rights" based approach to educational funding. Based on each student's unique needs funding, beyond the base funding, flows so that "the student" can meet the intended learning outcomes.

ADEQUATE

Find agreement on what constitutes an "adequate" level of educational programs and services in each and every school and fund them to that level. This approach does not differentiate along any lines, and each school would receive a base amount to provide an adequate education and nothing more.

EQUITABLE

Provide money in the form of specialized or categorical grants for targeted groups of students who belong to groups that have been identified as requiring additional support to succeed in school. Money flows to the additional programs and services beyond the ones available to all students in these targeted groups of students.

EQUAL

All students in the division - regardless of their advantage or disadvantage - are funded to a specific dollar amount of services and programs regardless of their educational needs. It's a fairly simple concept and goes beyond adequacy. This model reifes the already unequal playing field that exists in society where the privileged and unprivileged are pitted against each other.

Figure 3.3. Challenges to an Adequate, Equal, Equitable, or Appropriate Education

bulk of the revenues that flow into divisions and schools for such expenses as staff. Staff includes classroom teachers, school administrators (principals and vice principals), administrative assistants, librarians, and guidance counselors. Other expenses include textbooks, learning materials, and classroom equipment including such things as laboratory materials, art supplies, athletic equipment, and computers. Funding to heat, light, repair, and maintain the building, while not usually part of the revenues that come as the operational budget based on a strict student enrollment number, can depend in part on the student numbers, as they are oftentimes calculated using a formula based on occupancy rates (that is, the actual student enrollment divided by the maximum student population the school was built to educate). This is, of course, an illustrative example and as such is an incomplete list, but hopefully you get the idea.

Adequacy

The concept of an adequate education is a legalistic approach for ensuring that basic educational opportunities for all students exist whether advantaged or not based on the minimum requirements set forth in provincial/territorial legislation through an efficient, thorough, and uniform education system. Adequacy focuses on defining a minimum level of funding needed for every school to teach its students. The problem with adequacy is that it provides for education that is "just enough" rather than striving for one that is excellent.

Equality

Equality in education requires that school leaders provide the same resources, opportunities, and treatment to each and every student without regard to an individual's personal and social circumstances. For example, any social or academic disadvantage that may result from an individual's gender, ethnic origin, disability, or socioeconomic status should not be factored in when allocating financial resources to support educational programs and services. It has a constitutive element that implies that personal and social circumstances should not be taken into consideration when decisions are made about what services and programs ought to be funded. It presumes that all students are equal and ought to have the exact same level of school funding. The basic premise can be stated as, a student is a student, and as such all students deserve to be funded equally. It is a cookie-cutter approach that assumes that all children are equal without advantage or disadvantage.

Equity

Equity is not the same as equality; it is different from allocating the same amount of funding for every student. Fundamentally it is predicated on the belief that some groups of students need additional funding to serve them best. Funding equity presumes that particular groups of students, typically those belonging to protected categories that are enshrined in human rights legislation, require specialized educational programs and services that are specifically designed and delivered to them to make up for the social conditions that disadvantage them collectively and keep them from achieving their educational potential. It presumes that some categories of students are different, and therefore the goal of school funding is to provide differentiated levels of services and programs that meet their group's unique and collective needs.

Appropriateness

Appropriate education implies that each student should be offered a program of studies and the necessary support services that are designed and delivered to meet the individual's unique educational needs. It is about individuals and based on the legislative requirement that each student is guaranteed an education through access to the curriculum that allows that student to meet the grade-level standards established by the provincial or territorial jurisdiction. Its fundamental premise is: What is required in this specific instance to meet the unique learning needs of this child?

While for the purpose of this chapter the concepts have been separated, the truth is that they are almost always part of the fabric of the debates about how best to finance education. What is problematic in that admission, though, is that, without an ability to see them for what each one represents as a commitment that ought to drive financial considerations, it is difficult to understand what the basis for making financial decisions is and why decision makers are so passionate about their positions about what and what not to fund. It is not a matter of whose facts are correct but a contest of whose values matter most.

- **PRINCIPLE 3.5:** *Financial oversight is not optional.*
- **PRACTICE 3.5:** *Frequently and systematically monitor the flow of money to ensure that the financial transactions actually match the budgetary commitment in a timely manner.*

BUDGET CONSIDERATIONS

Before venturing into the discourse over who gets to control the budgetary decisions, it is important to recognize that there are some practices that ought to be enacted to shape conversations about who gets to decide what gets spent. One of the central challenges that plagues budget development for those who toil to develop budgets that are accurate, practical, and understandable is that mapping out the future is an imaginative exercise that cannot be done with precision. With such a limitation acknowledged up front, the likelihood of developing a budget that works can be increased if a few practices guide the process.

Budgets express how resources will be allocated and what measures will be used to evaluate an organization's progress to realize its priorities. Budget development is more effective when it is linked at the earliest stages to the school planning process and clearly connected to the school's priorities. Seeing both the planning and budgeting processes as equally important elements of a tangible commitment to the aspirations of a school community is essential if budgets are to be meaningful and priorities financially supported.

Budgeting is an iterative process that requires a series of revisions over a period of time—weeks and, more typically, months. It requires time to consult, research, make projections, and revise over and over again so that the budget estimates are both as accurate and as understandable as possible.

It is important that the authors of the budget not only produce documents that can be read and understood by experts and nonaccountants but that they also lead processes that make sense to the public that schools serve. If budgeting processes are secretive or shrouded in a mystical ceremony that only those who know the "secret handshake" understand, the public whose money is being expended will be suspicious, and rightly so. It is, after all, the public purse that is being spent.

Although it may be true that a single person in the organization is responsible for the overall assembly of the budget and its monitoring (typically this is the secretary-treasurer), no one person should be allowed to develop the budget alone or own it. Budgeting needs to be a collective responsibility in which a broad set of perspectives are considered by a group who can collaborate to develop a budget that reflects the aspirations of the school community.

Heraclitus of Ephesus, the ancient Greek philosopher known for his doctrine of change being central to the universe, is purported to have said: "Everything changes and nothing stands still." By developing budgets that can accommodate change, schools can respond to the very real challenges and opportunities that present themselves as the public changes its mind (as it frequently does) about what it expects schools to be able to do. Without getting into the silly tendency of "padding" a budget and then scurrying about at the end of a fiscal cycle to spend it, budget developers should design budgets with contingency lines to ensure that costs that are prone to unexpected price escalation are insured against unforeseen market forces.

RESPONSIBILITY AND BUDGETARY CONTROL

Educational finance, in general, can be described as the acquisition, alloca-tion, and management of funds to support formal educational institutions in terms of programs and services that enable students to be successful. Educa-tional leaders are responsible for developing and delivering on a financial plan that relates to the school's or division's priorities within an academic year and one that includes as an estimate the required expenditures together with the revenues available to ensure that all students are afforded the oppor-tunity to find success at school. This is no small feat.

Robert W. Smith and Thomas D. Lynch, the authors of *Public Budgeting in America*, describe public budgeting through four perspectives, which can be described as:

- THE POLITICIAN: sees the budget process as a political event conducted in the political arena for political advantage.
- THE ECONOMIST: views budgeting as a matter of allocating resources in terms of opportunity cost in which allocating resources to one consumer takes resources away from another consumer. The role of the economist is therefore to provide decision makers with the best possible information.
- THE ACCOUNTANT: focuses on the accountability value in budgeting that analyzes the amount budgeted to the actual expenditures, thereby describing the wisdom of the original policy.
- THE STEWARD: takes seriously the responsibility to manage, through revenue generation and targeted expenditures, the public purse—working tirelessly to earn the public's trust.

School leaders are asked to adopt all four of these perspectives in the work they do. It is not hard to find examples in which a principal has found her- or himself cast simultaneously as the politician, economist, accountant, and steward of public policy while still clinging, fundamentally, to the ideals that come with being an educator.

While not the only one worth considering, Smith and Lynch's perspective on a budget in a public policy context offers food for thought for educational administrators. For Smith and Lynch, a budget is a tool used to implement public policy. It is a plan, albeit one typically represented through numbers, that outlines how the available resources will be expended over a given period of time by an organization. It may well present possibilities for the acquisition of additional resources and ideally ought to provide a sense of the organization's financial well-being. A strong proposed budget will demon-strate how the makers of that budget had both an eye on the organization's financial health in the past fiscal period as well as what that might mean for the future.

The purpose of an educational institution's budget is to serve as an outline for expenditure distributions throughout the school year and delineate the priorities and determinations of decision-making authorities within the school district. Budgeting is a continuous process and incorporates planning, approving, and implementing an expenditure plan for the educational institution. Successful budget processes characteristically include input from all involved entities, guidance from administrators, strategic planning processes, management and reporting tasks, and rigorous administrative examination throughout the budget process. This is very similar to the work that principals undertake in trying to offer the appropriate levels of programs and services that students need to succeed.

It is important to note that, when budgets are applied to schools, as is the case with other public bodies, they have an economic, political, and technical basis. Unlike a pure economic theory, public-sector budgets are not entirely designed to allocate finite resources for the best economic use. Trying to calculate a "return on investment" on such a public good as education is impossible. If understanding how to apply pure economic theories to assess the costs of a formal education were easy, you would not need to read this chapter. As has been mentioned previously, defining the precise intended outcomes of a public education—a local, national, and international common good but one that also has private benefits—has proven to be an elusive endeavor and one that has been contentious and contested for decades.

It seems trite to advocate for the use of pure economic theories driven by the mantra of a "return on investment" to decide how best to determine and operationalize the school budget process. Not only do schools not produce products that can be assessed because their development is not complete even at graduation, but schools also play less of a role in shaping students' futures than do the combination of all of the factors beyond their control. However, they are technical elements of budgeting that are valuable in developing forecasts of the likely levels of revenues and expenses needed to operate schools.

ORGANIZATION OF SCHOOL BUDGETS

It is insufficient for school leaders to dramatically declare at a parent council or staff meeting that "the buck stops here" if the individual cannot demonstrate a decent understanding of how budgets are developed and the basic framework that holds them together. In order to be taken seriously as leaders, superintendents and principals need to have an understanding not only of the numbers contained in the budget but also of what the budget means as an organizational planning document that signals to the public where limited financial resources are being committed.

Budgets are controlling mechanisms that can limit and, in some cases, stop people from taking action and showing initiative. Far too often, thoughtful staff, teachers, and principals, all of whom have ideas on how to improve the educational opportunities of students, are heeled by the phrase "it's not in the budget." This phrase kills motivation. It is important to remember that valid ideas may have to exist for a time "outside" of the budget until the budget can accommodate them or new funding sources support them as part of a changed budget. Budgetary line items should not determine all of the actions schools take. Budgets, after all, have limited predictive power about what children need to succeed at school and are really just financial forecasts based on estimates and educated guesses.

BOTTOM-UP OR TOP-DOWN CONTROL

The approach to managing finances that a division or school adopts—be it centralized, decentralized, or a hybrid version—ought to reflect not only the organization's hierarchical structure but also its core values. The budgetary control of a school division normally reflects the pattern of authority and responsibility within the organization.

Exhortations to adopt financial decision-making approaches that do not align with how the other aspects of the organization are structured are doomed to cause confusion and frustration for school leaders who feel stymied by budgetary approaches as they try to make what they believe are financial decisions in the best interests of students. Without equivocating on the matter, it is imprudent to suggest that centralization of control and regulation by experts is the universal key that unlocks school improvement. Rather than searching for a single-minded quick fix, what is needed are thoughtful considerations that challenge the many antiquated financial frameworks that cripple schools by sticking to a nineteenth-century model of school financing that replicates the status quo but is never radically changed.

Both bottom-up and top-down budgets have their advantages and disadvantages. It is important to note, as Michael Fullan has asserted, that both top-down and bottom-up approaches to school budgeting can be drivers for school improvement. While bottom-up budgets can have a positive impact on employee morale because principals and teachers get to assume an active role in providing financial input to the budgeting process, they may vary greatly among schools within a single school division and create inequities within a single school system.

A bottom-up budget, also called participative budgeting, is a system of budgeting in which budget holders have the opportunity to participate in setting their own budgets. In this scenario, principals, typically with the support of a school team, prepare a school budget and forward it to central office for review and approval. Theoretically, or at least theoretically speaking, principals are assumed to have a better understanding of the specific financial needs of their schools than the central office administration. There is a general belief that creating a budget without the input of key personnel from the rank and file can result in underresourcing and underfunding a school or department. In addition, principals, department heads, and teachers may resent that their expertise and input is not valued in the budgeting process.

A top-down budget is one that is set without allowing the ultimate budget holder to have the opportunity to participate in the budgeting process. Budgets are prepared by top management and imposed on the lower layers of the organization. In top-down approaches, when senior management evaluates a school division's overall financial needs and compares the needs to projected revenues for a year, a clear picture of how much money can be reasonably allocated to different areas is formed in the minds of the senior managers. Decisions are made about where finances will have the most positive impact and staffers are given directives on what they have to work with. This approach allows senior management to maintain complete financial control over a budget. Top-down budgets clearly express the priorities and expectations of a school division's senior leadership and school board, but they can be unrealistic because in some cases they do not incorporate the input of the very people, principals and teachers, who are tasked with implementing them.

CAPITAL AND OPERATIONAL BUDGETS

Almost every organization has a capital and operational budget. While these two budgets are quite different in what they support—typically equipment and buildings (capital) versus programs and services (operations)—they are in fact linked to each other. Becoming familiar with each allows principals to better manage and lead a school's financial operations.

Capital Budgets

When you budget for capital expenditures, you are planning to invest in or purchase assets. In a school context, assets can include such items as expensive equipment (usually over a few thousand dollars) that is expected to last for more than a year and/or buildings and/or property. Capital budgets are normally associated with debt financing because the "draw" to make the purchase requires a large-scale or longer-term investment. Capital budgets do not fit "pay as you go" forms of taxation to pay for the expenditures. Assets, however, depreciate over time. Boilers break down, roofs develop leaks, and buses need to be replaced. Making a decision not to replace a capital asset is oftentimes not an option because schools need to be heated (or cooled), children need classrooms where water does not drip on their heads if they are to learn, and without a bus to get to school not much happens in terms of learning.

Operational Budgets

An operational budget is intended to cover a year's worth of "day-to-day" expenditures. Operational budgets typically include such expenses as employees' wages and benefits, plant operations and maintenance, and the purchase of items that are intended to last less than a year. Operational budgets are important because they indicate how much it costs to cover the expenses required to operate a school on a daily, but more realistically monthly, basis. Surpluses from operational budgets can be transferred to a "reserve fund" to pay for one-time operational expenses—sometimes a spike in the cost of a good or service—or the surplus can be transferred to the capital budget to defray the cost of specific projects that was not part of the long-term capital budget cycle.

BREATHING SPACE

Across the educational spectrum, it is not uncommon to hear stories about gifted school principals who have the uncanny ability to connect with students and families on a personal level. This quality should not be overlooked as an important characteristic of effective principals. But in order to serve those students and families well, those principals ought to be able to balance her or his school's annual budget.

It is unacceptable to turn a blind eye to principals who overspend their schools' annual operating budget, no matter how good she or he is at building relationships. The reality is that, to balance the budget and make up for the deficit created by one school principal who overspends each year, the district's finance staff must redistribute any surpluses from any of the other principals in the district who had been diligent with their school's funds. In effect, the "savers" lose whatever they believe they have in their school's "reserve funds" or "surplus" without knowing that the overall budget had to be balanced at the district level because the district only has one audited financial statement. All of the schools' surpluses must be drawn on to pay for one school's deficit.

Collegiality is a wonderfully normative concept until you find out that the new pay structure promised to your parent council has vanished because the bloke down the highway decided to bring a ventriloquist as part of his community engagement event.

A FRAMEWORK FOR BUDGETING

Many school leaders mistakenly assume that the only function of a budget is as an accounting document that records and reconciles revenues and expenditures. They ignore the fact that a budget reflects both a commitment to lead and a willingness to manage. A budget is obviously a management tool that can be used to determine who has authority in specific decision-making domains, but it is also a communication mechanism that offers a public view of a leader's competency as a financial steward. Budget formats establish the so-called rules of the game for budgeting and create a standard through which fiscal fidelity can be evaluated.

In reality, the budget format says a lot about how decisions are made in an organization. The manner in which the budget presents selected information illustrates how parts of the school district or school are interrelated or, in some cases, not. Budgets also demonstrate something about the organization's culture by indicating what initiatives get funded. While much energy has centered on arguments over whether centralized control over budgeting produces better school outcomes or not, very little attention has been invested to explain how some of the most common budget approaches used in schools and/or divisions impact operational decisions. While certainly not an exhaustive list, here are five school budget formats:

1. incremental line item
2. program-based
3. modified zero-based
4. priority-driven
5. performance-based

Incremental Line Item Budget

Arguably the simplest form of budgeting, incremental line item budgeting links the inputs of the system to the programs and services necessary to support school operations. These budgets typically appear in the form of accounting documents that express minimal information regarding purpose or an explicit objective within the system. It is a historical approach that uses past revenues and expenditures data as detailed by fund, function, or object. Figure 3.4 provides an example of how this type of budget can be used to operate a relatively small school.

The primary advantages of using an incremental line item budget are the simplicity and ease of preparation, the ability to organize by unit and object, its consistency with lines of authority and responsibility, and its allowance for accumulation of expenditure data by organizational unit for use in trend/historical analysis. The challenges are that it presents little useful information

Expenditure classification		Previous fiscal year budget (less 1.5%)	Current fiscal year budget	Next fiscal year budget (plus 2%)
Salaries & benefits	Teachers (10 fulltime teacher equivalents: also, referred to as "FTEs")	$738,750	$750,000	$765,000
	Principal (1 FTE)	$123,125	$125,000	$127,500
	Educational Assistants (4 FTE)	$73,875	$75,000	$76,500
	Administrative Assistant (1 FTE)	$29,950	$30,000	$30,600
Purchased services	Reading clinician (0.4 FTE)	$31,500	$32,000	$32,640
	Psychologist (0.2 FTE)	$19,720	$20,000	$20,400
Instructional materials, supplies and text books		$98,500	$100,000	$102,000
Non-capital expenditures (Less than $1000)		$9,850	$10,000	$10,200
Other		$19,720	$20,000	$20,400
Total		$1,144,990.00	$1,162,000.00	$1,185,240.00

Figure 3.4.   Small School Incremental Line Item Budget

to decision makers on functions and activities of organizational units, it does not include explicit justifications for expenditures, and it invites microman-agement by administrators without performance information.

It is possibly the most commonly used approach to develop a budget. The budget is prepared by taking the current period's budget or actual annual financial statement as a base to which incremental amounts are added to create the next cycle's budget. The budget committee therefore begins by asking the question: "What did we get last year?" To this figure is added a small increment, and that total sets the parameters for the following year's spending. The second question is: "What can we do this year if we receive this much more revenue?"

Program-Based Budget

Program-based budgeting is a financial structure in which money is allocated to a specific program or functional area based on the targeted services and activities offered within the program. This decision-making tool links the program under consideration to the ways and means of facilitating the pro-gram. It bases expenditures primarily on the general intended goals of a program and is less concerned with the specific elements contained in the program. Figure 3.5 offers an illustrative example of a budget intended to support the development of an indigenous language program.

Program element		Current fiscal year budget	
Staff salaries & benefits	Instruction (1.5 FTE Indigenous language teachers & 2 FTE Indigenous language educational assistants)	$240,000	$350,000
	Administration (0.5 FTE principal & 0.5 FTE administrative assistant)	$110,000	
Honoraria (Elders & community guest speakers)		$40,000	
Purchased services (Social Work and Speech-Language Clinicians)		$25,000	
Instructional supplies and materials (Indigenous language books & resources)		$10,000	
Land-based programming costs (transportation & fees)		$10,000	
Non-capital equipment (less than $1000)		$5,000	
Other (miscellaneous supplies)		$2,500	
	Total	$442,500.00	

Figure 3.5. Special Program-Based Budget

Program-based budgeting places less emphasis on control and/or evaluation measures within the budget because any reporting on the success of the program is summarized in broad terms and not in assessments of any specific line items. It therefore allows for more holistic long-range program evaluation and planning. The challenges of program-based budgeting include that assessments of its effects and effectiveness can be limited by changes in long-term goals, it assumes that there is general consensus on organizational goals, there can be a lack of adequate program and/or cost data, and it is difficult to administer programs that involve several organizational units with this type of budget.

Modified Zero-Based Budget

The basic tenet of the modified zero-based budget is that programs and services delivery levels must be justified annually during the development process. The modified zero-based budgeting approach begins with the premise that very little beyond the essential elements required for teaching and learning is so above critique that it justifies preapproval for funding.

Figure 3.6 illustrates how it might be used to allocate resources to support centrally administered information communication and technology services delivered at the local school level but managed at the district level.

In a school context, it is ludicrous to suggest employing zero teachers as an option. Thus, the traditional approach to zero-based budgeting must be modified to make the theoretical practically sound. The central thrust of this modified approach is the primacy that financial resources ought to be concentrated on the programs and services that are considered the core functions of schooling. Once this first consideration is accepted, the others are considered to be secondary, and the funding is built up by asking the question: What would happen if we allocated "zero" monies to this function?

Expenditure classification	Service impact	Budget consideration	Budget allocation
Centrally supported software licencing fees.	Support for teaching and learning are required by each school. This cannot be reduced.	Continuation of current funding level.	$40,000
Equipment (hardware replacement & repair).	While repairs cannot be delayed, the replacement schedule can be adjusted from 3 years to 4.	Budget can operate at 90% of current level; maintain 100% of current budget allocation for repairs but 75% of current budget allocation for replacement.	$25,000 repairs + $65,000 replacement $95,000
Salaries and benefits for central IT staff.	Currently 2.0 FTE IT technicians. This can be reduced to 1.5 FTE IT technicians with some loss of service response time.	Reduce staff and benefits by 25% of current budget allocation.	$156,000
Travel reimbursement for IT technicians when off-site to support school.	Reduced staff will still have to travel to the same distances as previous years.	Continuation of current funding.	$2,925
		Total	$293,925

Figure 3.6.   Information Communication and Technology (ICT) Modified Zero-Based Budget

A modified zero-based budgeting approach requires you to justify all planned expenditures for each budget cycle. The budget committee begins by asking the question: Is this initiative necessary to fulfill our core mission? It is followed by the question: What would happen if we did not fund it and offer this specific program or service?

Priority-Driven Budget

The philosophy of a priority-driven budgeting approach is that resources should be mapped on and allocated against a school's identified strategic priorities. This approach ensures that the highest-ranked priority gets fully funded before the second-highest, which in turn gets funded before the third ranked one.

Figure 3.7 is an example of how a school district can target resources to support its top three strategic priorities in rank order.

It ensures the finite amount of money allocated in the budget aligns with the priorities identified in a school's strategic plan. In overly simple terms, it involves (1) recognizing the financial resources available to the school district, (2) identifying the district's strategic priorities, (3) ranking the strategic

	Strategic priority	Initiatives	Current fiscal year budget
Higher	Improve school readiness	Provide subsidized voluntary full-day care and education for infants and toddlers (0-3 years) of siblings registered in the school district.	$500,000
		Develop partnerships with community-based health service providers in the areas of prenatal and early childhood (0-5 years), health care and basic maternal health services.	$100,000
	Increase graduation rates for students identified "at-risk" to not complete high school	Increase community-based learning opportunities.	$50,000
		Pilot an alternative schooling model for 20-25 grade 9 students identified as "at-risk" to not complete high school.	$250,000
Lower	Increase the number of students who achieve grade level performance in literacy and numeracy	Identify and articulate a common set of essential skills in reading, writing and mathematics for each grade level.	$50,000
		Ensure all teachers have access to necessary professional learning in these key areas.	$25,000
		Total	$975,000.00

(The left margin shows "Priority" with an arrow pointing from Higher to Lower.)

Figure 3.7.   Strategic Priorities-Driven Budget

priorities, and (4) allocating the available resources to the highest-ranked priorities until all of the monies are committed.

Priority-driven budgeting fixes the amount of school district resources and allocates the resources across the various programs based on their rankings. The budget committee asks two questions: (1) What are the priorities in rank order of importance? and (2) How much does it cost to fund each? When all of the money is gone, the budget is set.

Performance-Based Budget

Performance-based budgets estimate the costs associated with delivering programs and services and link these to a form of measurement or an evaluation of the programs' and services' outcomes. The programs and services are not ranked but are instead all considered worthy of consideration for funding.

Figure 3.8 is an example of how a school district can allocate resources for a district-wide instructional reading initiative and assess the effectiveness of the resources to make a positive impact based on anticipated key performance indicators.

The focus of this budgeting approach is on assessing whether or not the resources committed in the budget are supported by the resulting outcome. The assessment of the outcomes determines both the efficacy of the programs and services and any future budget commitments.

Performance-based budgeting focuses on results, and schools/departments are held accountable to certain performance standards. Performance and/or outcome assessment determines the efficacy of the programs and services. The budget committee begins by asking the question: Do the measurable outcomes that are achieved by funding this initiative match the cost of the investment?

CHOOSING A FRAMEWORK THAT WORKS

Many public-sector budget choices, as in the case of schools, will always be challenging, and hybrid models of five described approaches are no doubt often used. What needs to be understood better, however, is how the financial decisions made today that affect tomorrow align, or not, with the overall vision for both leading and managing a school's operations. A budgetary approach holds the potential to develop better estimates of the true costs of educating students. It also holds the power to control behavior. A budgetary approach can provide a framework for developing integrated plans that support school priorities and initiatives and can allow different parts of an organ-

Targeted area	Budget allocation	Process and/or outcome measures	Performance indicators
Interdisciplinary learning communities focused on reading across the curriculum	$20,000	New strategies developed by interdisciplinary learning communities to improve reading strategies. Creation of a pilot benchmark test for reading across the curriculum.	Creation of list of recommended reading strategies. Development of pilot benchmark reading test.
Divisional literacy coach for reading instruction	$100,000	Classroom visits by literacy coach. Teachers mentored by the literacy coach in the best practices for reading.	Increased student performance on local teacher-team developed reading assessment.
Development of reading recovery strategies	$30,000	Enhanced pedagogical knowledge of discipline-specific reading strategies. Interdisciplinary pilot programs and initiatives focused on improving reading.	Interdisciplinary learning communities' Final Reports.
Total	$150,000.00		

Figure 3.8.   Reading Initiative Performance-Based Budget

ization to be better coordinated, or they can stifle ingenuity and negatively affect morale.

Those responsible for the money needed to ensure that schools have the necessary financial resources to make good on their commitments to students and their families should also regularly assess whether the financial and human resources, including the time spent on the initiative, are allocated in such ways as to best position the school and/or division to achieve its educational goals.

It is not enough to develop a budget year after year and just follow it blindly. It is important to perform a postmortem at the end of the year to understand how well the budget performed. After the year is done, work needs to be undertaken to find an answer to the question: Did the operating budget allocate the necessary financial resources in the amounts that were required to provide the level of programs and services that students needed and that the organization committed to provide? A budget variance is a periodic measure used by governments, corporations, or individuals to quantify the difference between budgeted and actual figures for a particular accounting category.

A favorable budget variance refers to positive variances or gains; an unfavorable budget variance describes negative variance, meaning losses and shortfalls. Budget variances occur because forecasters are unable to predict the future with complete accuracy. As a result, some variance should be expected when budgets are created.

One of the objectives of budgeting is to provide a base against which actual results can be compared. Your budget must be realistic, as there is no point analyzing variances against an unrealistic budget. Variance analysis can be simply explained as planned versus actual. Budgets are too often proposed, discussed, accepted, and forgotten.

Variance analysis looks, after the fact, at what caused a difference between the planned revenues and expenditures versus the actual revenues and expenditures of an organization. When actual results are better than expected results, the resulting variance is described as a favorable variance. When actual results are worse than expected results, the variance is described as an adverse variance. Budget variances can happen for many reasons, including a faulty budget or simply differences between budget assumptions and actual outcomes. School leaders should examine all material on budget variances and every variance should stimulate questions. For example: Why did we overspend on reading recovery?

Two "big drivers" to budget variances are inflation and price (cost) escalation. These two can be explained as follows:

- Inflation is defined as a sustained increase in the general level of prices for goods and services. It is measured as an annual percentage increase. As

inflation rises, every dollar you own buys a smaller percentage of a good
or service. For example, if the inflation rate is 2 percent annually due to
the general increase in the cost of goods and services, that favorite two-
dollar cup of coffee is going to cost you an extra four cents (now rounded
to five in Canada because we gave up the penny) next year. Budgets need
to reflect inflationary projections.

• Cost escalation is defined as changes in the cost or price of specific goods
or services in a given economy over a period of time. It is caused by
substantial increases in the cost of important goods or services in which no
suitable alternative is available, and it tends to be a less-sustained price
increase. Based on the earlier example of your cup of coffee, if there is a
shortage of Arabica coffee beans next year, while the price of a coffee
should be $2.04, it might spike to $2.50 for a short period of time until the
shortage is dealt with.

Budgets are necessarily estimates. However, they serve schools best when
they are thoughtful and sound "best guesses" at the expected revenues and
expenditures of a fiscal period. No one expects perfection, even if we wish
for it. Budgets are by nature imperfect, just as are principals. However,
financial illiteracy should never be used as an excuse for poor financial
leadership and management.

• **PRINCIPLE 3.6:** *The public deserves to know how the money that was
collected has been spent.*
• **PRACTICE 3.6:** *Remember principle 3.1: In order for the public's trust
to be maintained, it is imperative that you can explain in plain language
how their money was spent.*

INTERNAL CONTROLS

Internal financial controls refer to the procedures adopted by the school or
division and implemented by central office administrators and school principals to detect errors, as mistakes do occur, or, in more serious cases, prevent
fraudulent use of public funds. The internal controls should also ensure that
there is accurate and timely reporting of financial information. In simple
terms, internal control can be described as a system—typically set in policies
and enacted through procedures—that helps make sense of how the money is
being spent on the various programs and initiatives that the school board or
local school council agreed it should be spent on. It provides a level of
assurance that the public's money did not vanish with nothing to show for it
in terms of student programming.

Accountability as a concept is actually a neutral term referring to being able to justify one's actions or statements. Yet because of a particular political climate that includes extreme suspicion about civil servants, and this includes school leaders, stewardship of public funds using the term "accountability" in the discourse of education is seen as inflammatory language and dangerous ground to tread on. Accountability in education is typically cast as one of the bogeymen intended to decimate the good work done in public education. Don't believe me? Just Google the phrase "accountability and education" and see where it takes you. Even though it is too often labeled pejoratively, in terms of school finance, plain and simple, accountability is important. It means that trustees, superintendents, and principals ought to

- respond periodically to questions concerning their financial decision making, including their choices of how and where they expend the public's money and where they collect revenues from, and
- be responsible for the exercise of financial authority that has been assigned to them.

Financial accountability is an inert concept until it becomes operationalized in the form of a single but complex question: Who is accountable for specific financial decisions and to whom are they accountable? Transparency underpins accountability.

Understandable financial information should be made available on a full (or at least as full as is legally permissible), regular, and timely basis to the public. Financial transparency is a fundamental element to developing an informed and educated school leadership team and to satisfying a discerning public who might be suspicious of those in leadership positions. Appropriate and meaningful participation by educational stakeholders, which includes a concerned public, should be welcomed and encouraged by those charged with the responsibility of caring for taxpayers' money. Information offered to the public provides them with a better understanding of what is required to finance the educational programs and services that students require to succeed in the ever-expanding globalized context that contemporary schools find themselves operating in.

Financial predictability is important for the overall operational performance of schools. A lack of predictability of the necessary financial resources to operate schools and offer programs and services undermines the efforts that go into making strategic priorities real in a tangible way. It can also make for an excellent alibi to hide poor performance behind "we couldn't provide the after-school mentoring we promised we would and that we know makes a profound positive difference for at-risk youth because there was no way to know if the funding was sustainable."

Ensuring a level of predictable funding does not mean that school leaders should make unconsidered financial commitments to programs and people that are beyond periodic review and, if deemed necessary, ended. Financial predictability is a relative concept that attempts to address the challenging task of being able to deal with financial uncertainty in the most appropriate manner. It is an approach that takes into account a province's, state's, or territory's fiscal context as well as the local financial outlook, which can change as a result of unforeseen global economic pressures.

Flexibility in financial decision making, in general terms, is an important factor that allows school leaders to achieve efficient, effective, and appropriate organizational performance at the level of the operational unit, which might be at the school or divisional level. Flexibility is premised on the belief that school leaders have the authority to make financial decisions and take the necessary actions within their defined area of responsibility.

Flexibility comes with the commitment that those making the decisions have developed enough financial competency and literacy so as to understand well the consequences of their choices and be able to explain the reasons behind their choices.

SUMMARY

The enduring dilemmas that accompany funding decisions, an endeavor so fundamentally important to civil society, challenge decision makers to get it as correct as is possible. Along a continuum of possibilities, school leaders have to balance calls to finance schools so that the least advantaged in society benefit the most, with the argument that schools need to be funded to maximize the greatest prospect of excellence. Should education be funded and distributed in such a way as to increase the likelihood that those whose prospects for living a good life would be otherwise bleak is improved and thus improve society overall? Or should schools be funded in such ways that those who have the greatest potential to benefit get access to the programs and services that will allow them to make meaningful contributions to society? It is hard to argue with either position, as both suggest that we will benefit as a society.

These are, however, the kind of concerns that never get discussed in earnest, and for some reason educational leaders are permitted to discuss the "dollars and cents" of education. Instead, we dither on about whether or not school-based or centralized budgeting better meets the needs of students. We worry about how much money is and is not in the system and fight over the size of the budget without examining the financial basics about how we are structuring the system. And school leaders rarely want to discuss money matters in public. They would rather not most of the time. The goal of this chapter is to improve the financial literacy of the readers and pose some fundamental questions about how we currently structure and approach school finance decisions with a hope that more gets placed on the table for consideration.

Chapter Four

Leadership Principles and Practices of Risk Management

> If a builder builds a house for a man and does not make its construction firm, and the house which he has built collapses and causes the death of the owner of the house, that builder shall be put to death.
> —Code Number 27 from the "Code of Hammurabi"; Hammurabi was a king of the Babylonian dynasty during the seventeenth century BC

In general, public-sector services exist in part to buffer society during turbulent economic, political, and social times. When it comes to launching new initiatives, if the potential outcomes are largely unknown or the risk exposure to the organization's members or the organization itself is deemed to be too high, it is reckless to throw caution to the wind and to be blinded by ambition and charge forward. School leaders must be able to recognize perilous hazards for what they are without completely stifling the urge to attempt to do something that might increase the likelihood for student and organizational success.

BREATHING SPACE

"Who would have guessed I would get sued over a deep fryer? Of all the crazy things for a principal to get sued over," James Bing whispered. "Really? A deep fryer?"

"Stop saying that. You are not being sued over a deep fryer," replied Lisa Haines, a midcareer vice principal.

Bing, a guileful veteran principal, shot back, "Sure as heck I am. People can say what they want, but all this is about is a deep fryer!"

In an attempt to keep the conversation collegial, Haines replied, "You drafted a contract with a for-profit cafeteria provider that guaranteed a minimum level of revenue if they paid for the cafeteria renovations. But in reality, you never got permission from central administration to sign it, let alone write it. You downloaded it from the Internet. Then when the new provincial Healthy Schools policy came in, you turned around at the last minute, after the renovations were complete, and told them, 'Oh by the way: No deep-fried food in the school. Too bad for you!' And now we have all been called here to get schooled by the superintendent on the division's insurance policies and indemnification vis-à-vis procurement and contracting services."

"It's not my problem that they have a lousy business plan that is based on selling kids crap," Bing said indifferently. "All I know is I saved the district seventy-five grand by getting Nacho-Dad to renovate the cafeteria. Now we have a brand new stainless steel commercial kitchen, and it's their job to figure out a better menu. I should get a bonus like they give out on 'Bay Street.' Anyway, the Nacho-Dads need to learn to read the fine print. I wrote in a clause that stated the contract could be revised in emergency situations. And don't tell me we do not have a crisis in childhood obesity. That is clearly an emergency."

Just then Superintendent Oxen walked over to the table Haines and Bing were seated at and asked Principal Bing for a minute of his time.

"Is it true that Jonathon Bong, your Advanced Placement chemistry teacher, lit the lab floor on fire last week?" inquired Oxen.

"Well, kind of. He does it every year. The kids love it. It's part of his strategy to increase student engagement. Those AP kids get bored easily. Every year he wows his class by setting the floor on fire during a lesson," Bing responded.

Oxen repeated the phrase slowly and incredulously: "The floor catches fire."

"No, no, it doesn't really catch fire. It's the liquid methane that catches fire," Bing explained.

"He lights methane on fire?" asked Oxen.

"Well, you know, it's a liquid, and as it boils, it releases a flammable gas. So on the first day of class each year, Bong pours the contents of the test tube onto the floor and a huge puddle of fire appears. Students gasp in horror but love it. Spreading across the floor, the specks of fire appear to dance on the surface before they quickly burn out. It is very cool," said Bing. "You're not telling me one of his students complained, are you? They love it. Babies!"

"No, it wasn't one of Bong's students who contacted my assistant. It seems that some of the liquid vapor slid through a small crack in the flooring and seeped into the cafeteria below. It splashed the blue-haired lady who works the grill at Nacho-Dad, and her hair caught on fire. She's suing the school division for two million dollars. And maybe we should talk about the deep fryer while we are at it?" replied Oxen.

- **Principle 4.1:** *Learning necessarily involves uncertainty.*
- **Practice 4.1:** *Always take a measured approach to balance the level of risk against the potential for success afforded by taking a leap of faith.*

A RISKY START

There is no way around it: The reality is that education is a risky business. This risk begins the moment that parents allow their young children to attend school for the first time. In some ways, over a period of at least the twelve years they spend in a partnership with a school, that anxiety they felt on the first day never fully disappears. They are permitting other people, almost complete strangers, to raise their children.

Parents, however, take a chance so that their child can successfully navigate a world they have very little ability to control and one in which they cannot ultimately decide what will occur next. They take a risk hoping that their child will return home at the end of the day whole and maybe slightly better off having experienced all that is school. They accept the risk, even with the uncomfortable knots in their stomachs, as they wave goodbye at the kindergarten classroom door because they believe two things: (1) that the risk is worth the benefit and (2) that those who act in loco parentis will do whatever they can to minimize their child's exposure to undue levels of risk that might bring about harm while offering their children some opportunities to grow that they themselves might not be able to offer.

Parents trust that the teacher will stand, in relation to their child who has now become someone else's "student," in a position of authority similar to the one they hold and act as a prudent and caring parent would—as an unofficial guardian. It is an uneasy moment for many parents, but the education system requires that they trust the people who work in schools will do right by their child. Parents are mostly concerned with the "human risk" factors of school, that is, the risk factors that might harm any people during the school day, especially their own children. But there are other risk categories that school leaders must manage, including the legal, reputational, and financial risks associated with every decision made every day. All of these areas are interrelated and have far-reaching implications when not attended to with diligence.

At an operational level, the negative outcomes of a lack of leadership of the risk inherent in operating schools can be both far-reaching and deep. Figure 4.1 illustrates some of the negative outcomes that can come when leaders do not take risk seriously.

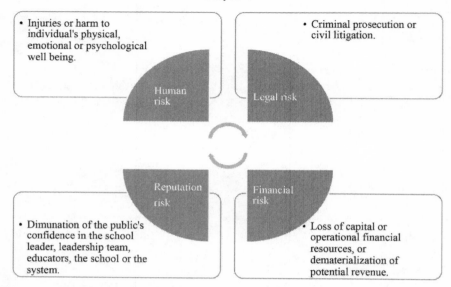

Figure 4.1.   Risk Exposure Quadrants

Setting lofty goals for school success and committing the human and financial resources required to pursue them is a noble venture. Leadership, however, comes with the responsibility to consistently assess the exposure to operational risks that could cripple the school and, worse, quite literally the people who occupy it.

- **Principle 4.2:** *While trust without risk is an oxymoron, demanding blind trust without offering reassurances is willful ignorance.*
- **Practice 4.2:** *Earn the trust of colleagues, parents, and the public by not recklessly exposing them to unnecessary perils.*

RELATIONAL TRUST

"It's a vice to trust all, and equally a vice to trust none." This sentiment from the letters of first-century Roman statesman and philosopher Seneca to Lucilius illustrates what some parents felt when they wiped away their tears and left their child with an adult who is, at first, a stranger. Trust always involves a gamble: a gamble that something worthy will transpire during the school day but uneasiness that the school day also involves risk. Parents count on the fact that those responsible for teaching their children have calculated the risk their child might be exposed to and have done their best to mitigate the negative effects that may accompany the risky business of schooling.

Trust is also a fundamental element of leadership. School leaders—any leaders for that matter—can no longer trust that people will comply with their wishes simply by virtue of the formal authority the leaders hold. Nowadays the power of authority is all too often questioned and challenged, and for good reason. News headlines inundate us daily with tales of leaders who abused their power. In light of this, what successful leaders need to rely on is the power associated with trust and being trusted when they have earned that by acting prudently.

The books about educational leadership too often talk about "trust" as if it were a singular thing—it is not. In highly clinical terms, trust is a relationship established between a "trustor" and a "trustee." Trust requires something from both parties, and this is true not only of interpersonal trust but also of trust between people and institutions. In fact, it has been suggested that the lack of trust in many of our traditional social institutions is now best characterized by the never-ending howls for accountability and transparency in which people say, "Not only do I want to know what you are doing, but I also need to see it with my own eyes to believe you are really doing it." It is tantamount to admitting that I cannot trust what you tell me or what I cannot verify with my own eyes.

Do not take for granted the fact that the public these days wants to be given a reason to trust those who lead. Such a requirement of proof flies in the face of what the traditional education system has required of families. Trust has been taken for granted, and the new norms of having to earn trust are challenging educators to rethink how they relate to parents and the public. Many educational leaders are perplexed and feel a sense of affront when confronted with the realization that part of their job is to earn something that used to be automatic, that is, basic trust.

The role of the "trustor" in the formal schooling of children requires a parent to take risks by virtue of trusting another person without knowing much about that individual. Think back to the earlier example of the first day of school. The role of the "trustee"—in this case the school staff—is to be trustworthy and continuously act in ways that earn parents' and the public's (the "trustors") trust. When each party is decently good at its designated role, a state of trust results. This trust is not forever, and each party needs to be conscious that trusting relationships require effort and vigilance. If either party falls down on the job or lets the other party down, trust can diminish and, in some cases, disappear.

Trust is not a soft, elusive concept that you either "do" or "do not" have. Real trust is earned. Trust is earned in part by being reliable, in which reliability refers to the extent to which students, staff, and parents can depend on you to come through for them, to act consistently, and to follow through with commitments you have made.

Professors Anthony Bryk and Barbara Schneider from the University of Chicago studied the reform efforts in four hundred Chicago-area schools and underscored the central role that relational trust plays in binding a school's staff to a collective commitment to schoolwide student success initiatives. Professionally speaking, relational trust can be described as the mutual understanding we hold when those of us invested in the hard work of educating children uphold a shared and candid understanding of the obligations we have in our roles as teachers, administrators, and support staff to support students. We hold our colleagues to the expectations associated with their roles, and when they live up to them, good things happen for children.

Relational trust is also correlated to competence. Similar to reliability, seeming competent has to do with their belief in your ability to perform the tasks required by your formal leadership position. For example, if a principal means well but lacks the necessary management knowledge, skills, or acumen, that principal may be well liked but is not likely to be trusted to do the job. Trust is also correlated to integrity, character, and authenticity, which are all dimensions of relational trust. Your school community does not expect perfection, but they do expect that you can be counted on to represent situations fairly.

Open communication allows relational trust to become stronger. Judgments about openness have to do with how freely they feel you shared information with them. They do not expect you to tell them every gory detail of what was said at a staff meeting, but highly guarded communication, for instance, provokes distrust because people wonder what is being withheld and why.

POWER AND RESPONSIBILITY

In short, school leaders have a lot of powers. Superintendents and/or directors of education, principals, and school boards each have significant powers assigned to them under the provincial legislation, typically within an Education or School Act, which governs the formation and operation of schools and districts in a particular jurisdiction. In exercising your powers, you can either enhance and strengthen or reduce and suppress the rights, opportunities, and expectations of each member of the school community, whether they are students, teachers, or parents.

Author Ray Bradbury is quoted as saying in an interview with the *New York Times*, "If we listened to our intellect, we'd never have a love affair. We'd never have a friendship. We'd never go into business. Well, that's nonsense. You've got to jump off cliffs all the time and build your wings on the way down." People confuse the personal with the professional, so a caveat is offered on two intricately connected exceptions that are worth noting: love and trust. In such cases, please feel free to take a leap of faith into the unknown.

A serious problem transpires, though, when educational leaders take Bradbury's words literally without exception and begin to advocate for high-risk initiatives without seriously considering who—besides themselves—are being exposed to risk. It is morally reprehensible and legally wrong to put someone else at risk without their knowledge of the risk, the consequences of exposure, and their full consent. Yes, this is a burdensome process, but respectful engagement requires it.

Risk, in a very simple way, can be defined as the probability of an event and its consequences. Typically, risk management is regarded as the practice of using processes, methods, and tools for managing the risk associated with the outcomes of operational decisions. In a school context, leadership is concerned with setting parameters about what kinds of risk should be taken to improve student success, assessing the risks and identifying harms that might result when initiatives go awry, implementing strategies to mitigate these undesired effects, and communicating to the public why the risks are worth taking.

To be blunt, no matter what the mind-numbing jingles suggest, as an educational leader you do not have the privilege of building your wings as your innovative idea nosedives into the hard ground below because it is rarely you who risks being injured. Rather it is, more often than not, the students or teachers whose well-being is jeopardized. Leadership is about taking responsibility for the welfare of others and not exposing them to unnecessary harm while you are pursuing your dreams to "be the change" you wish to see.

- **Principle 4.3:** *No human being can possibly foresee all of the consequences of an innovative disruption, no matter how obvious those consequences may appear in hindsight.*
- **Practice 4.3:** *Look for "foolproof" approaches to risk management, which means that any approach to assess the potential for organizational ruin is only as good as the competency and character of those charged with leading the organization.*

ORGANIZED UNCERTAINTY

Since the 1980s, and perhaps extending back a decade or so earlier, expectations associated with risk management in school contexts have undergone a dramatic expansion in their scope and importance. From planning and executing field trips that return every single student safely intact to protecting students from enduring the psychological harm associated with bullying, principals must be aware of the need to develop a contingency mindset—a blueprint of sorts for thinking—to deal not only with the outcomes of what can be lightheartedly termed but, perhaps accurately so, as the organized chaos we call school.

It is important to pay careful attention to the caution offered by Yehezkel Dror that there is at any given moment a high probability of low-probability events occurring. In other words, "surprise dominates." The essayist, scholar, philosopher, and statistician Nassim Nicholas Taleb, in his book *The Black Swan: The Impact of the Highly Improbable*, proposes that events such as these manifest themselves as "black swans." Black swans are events, positive or negative, deemed improbable yet causing massive consequences. They are events that by nature are almost impossible to predict. But they are also known hazards, such as floods, hurricanes, or earthquakes, that, owing to the low likelihood of occurrence or the high cost of mitigating action, remain as the episodic occurrences that leaders seem to be consistently over- or under-prepared for when they do transpire. There are also crises such as pandemics that typically unfold over weeks, months, or a few years for which the scope or timing remains unknown even with preparations.

In organizational continuity and risk management, a business sustainability plan is only one part of the process that prepares an organization to respond coherently to an unplanned event and maintain business operations. Thus, the business operations sustainability plan is important, as it can act as a reference guide. Without going into great detail, a sustainability plan should cover such areas as:

- Conducting a business impact analysis (BIA) that takes into consideration the impact of some specific and foreseeable, however unlikely, catastrophes. For example, what impact would the loss of the school's computer systems' server have on the school's operations if it went down for a day or two or longer?
- Establishing plans, measures, and arrangements for business operations continuity. For example, what are the "work-arounds" or "work-throughs" that can be enacted in a timely fashion, and for how long could they be sustained without exhausting staff?
- Establishing readiness procedures. For example, is there an assessment of how ready the staff is to enact the sustainability plan measures? Do staff know there is one, and what needs to be done in the unlikely event that [fill in the blank] occurs?
- Finally, creating a procedure for auditing and assessing the sustainability plan as things change.

While school leaders must address and deal with these to maintain some level of school operational sustainability, equally important will be their ability to provide leadership that offers a calming effect and creates in the minds of students, staff, and parents the idea that the school community is a safe place.

ACCEPTING HUMAN ERROR

Every day each one of us makes personal decisions concerning our acceptable level of risk. We do it when we decide where to live, what type of vehicle to purchase, or whether to buy life insurance or a homeowner's policy. We also determine the risk we are willing to accept and able to afford when we set the deductible limits for our automobile insurance policies. The same is true of elected officials making decisions during their annual budget process when they weigh their constituents' competing demands for services versus their willingness and/or ability to pay taxes. The balance between risk and resources involves policy decisions. It involves making tough decisions about public needs and public funding. The economic reality is that most communities are either unable or unwilling to bear the cost of providing enough resources to fund every possible scenario. To do so would mean that schools, fire, police, public works, and other essential services could not be adequately funded. As frustrating as it might be to a risk-reduction leader, funding is both an economic and a political decision. The community is willing to accept the gap or deficiency known as the acceptable level of risk. However, there are a few typical human-error types that have an impact on managing and assessing risk in a school context:

- SLIP

A slip is a simple frequently performed physical action that goes wrong. For example, you type out a somewhat curt, what others might consider overly critical, email to vent your frustration about the school board's recent decision to reduce funding for the subsidized lunch program for low-income families who hover just above the official "low-income cutoff" number and do not technically qualify for the program. You begin to type out your principal colleague's name "Jane" but do not pay any attention to what the "auto-type" function did. You hit send, feel better, and head home. The next day you are called to the superintendent's office because you emailed "Janice," the chair of the school board's finance committee.

- LAPSE

We are all prone to have a lapse of attention or memory. Perhaps, as part of the onboarding process for new hires, it is your responsibility to collect their banking information and forward it to the folks in the payroll department in central office. One time after a particularly taxing week, you decide to wait until the following week to send in the forms. But as will happen far too often, the following week is even more frenetic than the previous one. The forms never get sent in and suddenly you are dealing with a staff member who has not been paid and cannot make rent because he survives paycheck to paycheck.

- MISTAKE

A mistake is caused by not properly understanding how something works or by an error of diagnosis or planning. For instance, as part of the due diligence you are required to complete with new hires, you are responsible for contacting three professional references to ask some specific questions about the candidate's suitability. You manage to contact two but are having difficulty getting a hold of the third, which happens to be the individual's current workplace supervisor. You have left messages, but no one has returned your calls. However, you decide to make the recommendation to hire based on the two completed reference checks that seemed relatively positive. Three weeks after the new hire starts to work in your school, you hear from a professional acquaintance that your new colleague was terminated from his previous position for theft.

- VIOLATION

A violation is a deliberate breach of rules and procedures. By way of an example, imagine that the school is getting by on a virtually nonexistent information communication technology budget, and the one place that has been squeezed to the limit has been the upgrade of existing software. Someone you met at a professional development conference mentioned that it is possible to download educational programs and software for free through a third-party provider. Even though you know it is against district policy, you download the material anyway because kids deserve access to twenty-first-century learning tools. The next day the network system administrator sends out an email to all staff informing them that a computer virus has been unleashed and is wreaking havoc, which will result in thousands of dollars needing to be spent to resolve the problem.

The truth is that human error is both universal and also inevitable. No one expects you to be perfect in everything you do. Try not to lose sleep over your imperfections—seriously. That said, the public expects you to have taken serious care to assess the dangers associated with mass education to ensure that some of society's most vulnerable citizens are as well protected from harm as they can be.

- **Principle 4.4:** *Leadership is about encouraging innovative and novel approaches to education without exposing the organization to the likelihood of ruin.*
- **Practice 4.4:** *Effectively leading risk is not about avoiding all risk, nor is it about seeking out unnecessary risk. Leadership is concerned with making deliberative operational decisions based on assessments that what might be gained outweighs what could be lost.*

LOOSELY COUPLED ORGANIZATIONS

Managing a school's operations is a bit like treading on a tightrope, at least at times. And leading a successful school can be doubly so. It is very difficult to make the bold decision to try something different—something truly innovative—with respect to the operational aspects of the school without rocking the boat too much and challenging a status quo that has become entrenched in the discourse of "but this is how we do things around here."

In many regards, schools were originally conceived of and organized to operate as conservative social institutions. Recall that they were established to help transmit the values of a community to the next generation of community members. They were not intended to be enterprises that pushed the boundaries of conventionality through social innovation. Understanding why schools are somewhat impervious to operational change is important but should not be disheartening.

The fear of failure can be, and in some instances should be, a sign that exposure to some risks needs to be seriously considered and reconsidered before decisions are finalized and enacted. It is fundamentally important that leaders find a balance between the risks that come with innovation and the need to conserve the trust that is placed in the educational system and those who lead it.

Without pretending that it is the archetypal definition, risk can be understood as anything that might happen and, if it did happen, would have a positive or negative impact on a school or school division for accomplishing its educational mandate. And risk is a central component to innovation, which in turn fuels the engine of school improvement initiatives. Across public-service sectors, leaders are encouraged to take risks and not yield to the paralytic temptation to avoid failure at all costs.

It seems appropriate at this juncture to offer a caveat. Parents and the public in general have no appetite whatsoever for you subjecting their children to a series of failed instructional experiments veiled in the lexicon of twenty-first-century schooling. For the sake of educational innovation, students should not be forced to endure constant flops and fails in the classroom. Perhaps it is time to suggest that you return to and reread the opening interlude of the chapter on personnel leadership. There is an attempt to impress upon you a certain point. In the classroom, the opportunity to fail in teaching effectively should not be considered an option.

That said, however, in operational aspects of how we organize and run schools, innovation should be welcome. The bottom line is that all innovations involve an assessment of the tradeoffs between risk and return. To minimize risk and unintended consequences, school leaders need to understand how to make informed choices when it comes to new programs and services and new models of funding them. Leaders need to adopt a mindset that permits them to examine the evidence that an innovation is worth the effort rather than just relying on whims and the fickleness of gut instinct.

It is also worth heeding the caution offered by T. S. Eliot, who said, "Always remember you're unique; just like everyone else." There is all too often an assumption that innovations in schools need to be uniquely designed for a particular jurisdiction because the local context is different. It leads to the immediately negative rejection of potentially great ideas simply because the idea was "not built here." Leadership can come from the ability to find and duplicate a successful innovation from a neighboring jurisdiction, even if such an approach does not have the same cachet as pioneering an innovation. Adopting a successful innovation from another site requires enough humility to set aside the need to be the author of a new program and enough courageous commitment to manage a meaningful change. There is no doubt that safety is found in applying an incremental approach and simply tinkering around the margins of how we operate schools. Such an approach seems justified if school leaders are satisfied with the status quo. Innovation, whether borrowed from other successful programs or invented on site, is not for the faint of heart, as it requires that leaders face the political intolerance that is concomitant with taking risks and making mistakes. The backlash that can accompany innovation requires a robust understanding of how the change affects the people and finances committed to schools.

- **Principle 4.5:** *The most detrimental operational outcomes ought to come from the places you least expect them to and in forms that you least expect them to take.*
- **Practice 4.5:** *Leadership is about avoiding any foreseeable disastrous outcomes of bad decisions while preparing the organization to "roll with" the unlikely but tolerable negative outcomes that ensue. Leaders need to provide and maintain the energy and commitment required to absorb the rare "blind-side" hits that no one could predict.*

THE VIEW FROM THE CROW'S NEST

Given the number of times that school leaders are inundated with the metaphor of changing the organizational direction of a school being somewhat akin to trying to turn a large ship, it is worth recalling that, prior to the advent of radar the crow's nest was the common structure in the upper part of the main mast of a ship used as a lookout point. This position ensured the best view for lookouts to spot approaching hazards, other ships, or land.

It seems as if the frequency of "high-impact, low-probability" (HILP) macroevents in the past two decades signals the emergence of a new "normal." Apparent large-scale, one-off, high-profile crises such as 9/11, Hurricane Katrina, the British Petroleum oil spill in the Gulf of Mexico, and the Japanese earthquake and subsequent tsunami, were all megadisasters requiring rapid responses at a global level, marking the beginning of what has been termed a "crisis trend."

BREATHING SPACE

The 2010 British Petroleum oil rig disaster that was depicted in the Academy Award–nominated film *Deepwater Horizon* serves as a case study of how latent errors, enabling conditions, and a lack of management acumen can blind leaders to the potential for tragedy. The events that led up to the catastrophe are well chronicled but can be categorized as ignoring early warning signs, relying on outdated failsafe technologies to solve problems that might occur, and believing that the survival of near misses was actually a sign of successful management practices fed into the overinflated hubris of the leadership team. The combination of these factors can be illustrated in the following algorithm:

Latent Errors + Enabling Conditions × Untamed Ego = Organizational Catastrophe

When leaders get caught up in their ego, their untamed ego erodes their effectiveness as decision makers. The combination of false pride and hidden self-doubt created by an unchecked ego feeds into a distorted image of self-importance. Very few school leaders are willing to admit that they have big egos. In fact, many want to suggest that they have no ego at all, lest they be labeled a narcissist. There is little doubt that one critical feature of effective school leadership is humility. In the book *The One Minute Manager*, author Ken Blanchard states, "People with humility do not think less of themselves; they just think about themselves less."

However, coupled with humility is the need for positive or healthy narcissism. Healthy narcissism is a quality that comes from having a realistic self-image of one's own inherent value without being cut off from one's inner emotional state. In order to be of service to others, a school leader should believe that she or he has something of value to offer her or his students or school community that might make a positive impact on their well-being. This sense of not only being of service but also being capable to serve is a healthy form of narcissism that says: "Yes, I am important enough that I can make a difference in someone else's life."

A MINDSET FOR THE UNTHINKABLE

Schools are not immune from the effects of high-impact, low-probability events. Whether it is the unimaginable violence that tragically erupts on a campus in the case of a school shooting or the damage to a school that can occur as the result of a fire, flood, or tornado, the public perception is that, because these crisis events seem to be occurring with increasing frequency, school leaders should be prepared to deal with the upheaval and stress that accompany them. It is a matter of trust.

The public trusts that in some way school leaders are prepared for the inevitable crisis. It is under this kind of public scrutiny that leadership is judged. In the quiet of the coffee shop or on Facebook, people will ask: How did the principal react to the crisis and was this good enough? It is simply impossible to plan for every crisis. Many are unpredictable. That is why the episode turns into a crisis. Not expecting, however, that you will face a crisis of some sort during your tenure as principal seems foolish. While it might be true that in some rare cases it is impossible to foresee an organizational tsunami before it hits, school leaders can rely on some management norms to better position their schools to weather the storm.

- Recognize that high-pressure situations create enabling conditions for organizational disaster. Leaders need to examine their and their staff's decision making during pressure-filled time periods and ask the question: If I had more time and resources, would I make the same decision?
- Research demonstrates that when leaders become numb to the statistical risk associated with the outcomes of the decision at hand, they become less concerned with the level of risk even though the likelihood of negative consequences remain the same.
- Unless expressly required to consider worst-case scenarios, many leaders will not give serious thought to the potential hazards of their actions.
- When organization-level decisions produce poor outcomes, it is important to conduct a "post-mortem" of what went wrong to determine the root causes, learn from them, and teach others about the lessons that can be learned.

Educational leaders are lauded at conferences for their success and are championed as trailblazers whose ideas are worthy of a platform to preach from and typically attract a bevy of followers. There is nothing inherently wrong about celebrating success. However, it is extremely rare, especially given the rhetoric of learning from failure, to see school leaders put on full display an experiment gone awry so that others might learn from their experience. In learning organizations like schools, leaders should require that as much emphasis be placed on dissecting failures as there is on heralding success.

SCHOOL OPERATIONAL RISK EXPOSURE (SOREs)

A school operational risk exposure analysis (see figure 4.2) offers an illustrative model, albeit a somewhat simple one, that allows principals to consider both the likelihood of a negative outcome that might result in making a specific operational decision that has a level of risk associated with it and the potential impact on the school's operations that are associated with the risk exposure.

Erika Hayes James, an organizational psychologist at the University of Virginia's Darden Graduate School of Business, and Lynn Perry Wooten, a clinical associate professor of strategy, management, and organizations at the University of Michigan's Ross School of Business, in their book *Leading under Pressure: From Surviving to Thriving before, during, and after a*

		Likelihood of a Negative Outcome		
		Highly improbable	Improbable but potentially possible	Highly probable and likely possible
Impact of Negative Outcome	Significant	Those very rare events that no one could see coming but can cripple a school's operations.	Events that transpire that were unlikely to occur but can be crippling.	A blind donkey could have seen these coming and would have avoided at all costs.
	Moderate	Those very rare events that no one could see coming that with time and energy can be recovered from.	Events that transpire that were unlikely to occur but ones that can tax organizational energy.	Foreseeable events that can be survived but call into question your masochistic tendencies.
	Minor	Those very rare events that no one could see coming that act as speed bumps.	Events that transpire that were unlikely to occur and have very little impact.	Foreseeable events that come with the business of running schools.

Figure 4.2.   SORE Analysis Matrix

Crisis identify two primary types of organizational crises: "sudden" and "smoldering."

Sudden crises are circumstances that occur without warning and beyond an institution's control. Consequently, sudden crises are most often situations for which the institution and its leadership are not blamed. Alternately, smoldering crises begin as minor internal issues that, due to a manager's negligence, develop to crisis status. It is commonplace that, in the immediate period after the smoldering of the crisis has dissipated, leaders are questioned for not having a plan in place to deal with crisis management and are held responsible to any subsequent negative effect on the institution that is a result of not being prepared.

The capability to lead under extreme pressure can be described as crisis leadership. Crisis leadership matters precisely because crisis events are inevitable. Crisis leadership matters because leaders of organizations can make a difference in the extent to which people are affected by a crisis. Crisis leadership matters because in its absence the stakeholders who are adversely affected by the crisis cannot truly recover from the damaging event. Crisis leadership matters because, despite the damage that is caused by a crisis, effective leadership is the one factor that creates the potential for a school community to recover following the crisis and the possibility that the community might be stronger than it was before the crisis.

James and Wooten identify five essentially inevitable conclusions we can draw about crises—whether current or from times past—and the rippling effect they can and have had. First, crises are inevitable. Some crises may be avoided, and some may be managed well enough to limit long-term damage, but at the end of the day, every organization, and in fact every nation, will experience one or more crisis of some magnitude. Second, it is often the handling of a crisis that leads to more damage than the crisis event itself. Third, effective crisis leadership involves much more than good communication and public relations. Although these certainly help, rhetoric and positive spin alone will not resolve a crisis. Fourth, learning from a crisis is the best hope we have of preventing repeat occurrences. Finally, crisis events can create potential for significant opportunity to be realized for individuals and for organizations.

At its core, crisis leadership, or the ability to lead under pressure, requires that a particular leadership frame of mind, accompanied by a key set of behaviors, be present. The frame of mind needed to manage crises well is characterized by openness to new experiences, willingness to learn and take risks, an assumption that all things are possible, and a belief that even in times of crisis people and organizations can emerge better off after the crisis than before. Clearly, crises are traumatic, and I don't want to leave a false impression or indicate that there is not real pain and suffering that results from them. Indeed, this can be, and often is, the case. Leading in times of crisis means we must address and deal with these circumstances. Our goal, however, is to emphasize that leadership is also about creating possibilities so organizations can blossom in ways that might not have been predicted or possible in the absence of the pressures that crises evoke.

Thus far, what has been presented can be categorized as the human, legal, financial, and reputational costs potentially incurred when risks taken do not turn out well. These costs can range from miniscule or negligible to enormous or even insurmountable. Sometimes a single small short-term risk leads to a disastrous and costly outcome. Sometimes a seemingly large risk turns out well for all. Sometimes accumulating, overlapping, long-term risks lead to a full-blown crisis. Crises based on too much risk taking are considered crises that could have been avoided. As I described earlier, however, crises and the costs that are incurred due to crises are sometimes unavoidable and are not, in all cases, caused by accumulating risks. Natural disasters, random violence, and hazards we are ignorant of can all create unforeseen crises we then need to manage.

THREE RISKIER AREAS

What are the areas that pose the most risk for school leaders? It turns out that most crises tend to occur within one or more of these three operational arenas: employment of personnel, finance, and facilities and property. Figure 4.3 lists three particularly risky operational areas that can typically lead to operational conundrums and lays out what leaders need to pay attention to in creating their risk management plan.

INDEMNIFICATION

Because schools cannot guarantee that disaster will never strike, they need to take steps to indemnify themselves appropriately. While school leaders are not expected to be experts in the insurance industry, they should be aware of and ensure that adequate levels of insurance exist so as to protect the school division, its students and staff, and others who it comes into contact with who may suffer an injury or harm while on school premises or while operating under the auspices of the school's authority.

A basic understanding of insurance coverage is quite simple. Typically, a school division purchases insurance to indemnify itself and its employees against loss or peril. In the event of a claim, the insurance company pays its insured client for injuries and losses. The insurance company may then sue the party that the injured person contends caused the damages. However, as anyone who has filed an insurance claim knows, the insurance transaction rarely transpires with that kind of ease.

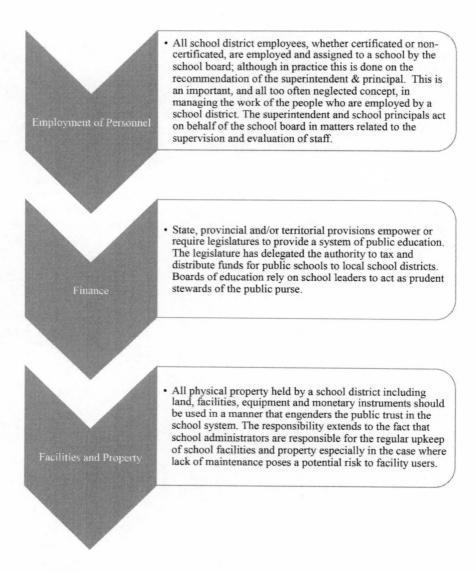

• All school district employees, whether certificated or non-certificated, are employed and assigned to a school by the school board; although in practice this is done on the recommendation of the superintendent & principal. This is an important, and all too often neglected concept, in managing the work of the people who are employed by a school district. The superintendent and school principals act on behalf of the school board in matters related to the supervision and evaluation of staff.

Employment of Personnel

• State, provincial and/or territorial provisions empower or require legislatures to provide a system of public education. The legislature has delegated the authority to tax and distribute funds for public schools to local school districts. Boards of education rely on school leaders to act as prudent stewards of the public purse.

Finance

• All physical property held by a school district including land, facilities, equipment and monetary instruments should be used in a manner that engenders the public trust in the school system. The responsibility extends to the fact that school administrators are responsible for the regular upkeep of school facilities and property especially in the case where lack of maintenance poses a potential risk to facility users.

Facilities and Property

Figure 4.3. Risky Operational Areas

BREATHING SPACE

Let me offer a benign example. While out on a camping trip with the grade 12 class, Boris, the outdoor education teacher, built a campfire. He knew it was too large for the fire pit but wanted to impress the sometimes jaded high school seniors because he considered himself the school champion of "engaged learning." However, while Boris the Engaged was demonstrating how to eat a s'more while blindfolded, the campfire got out of control and started a grass fire that spread to the national park's interpretive building. Sadly, the interpretive building was rendered charred ruins.

Good Hands Insurance Company, which has insured the interpretive building, paid the National Parks Commission the estimated cost of reconstruction of the building and then sued Boris's employer, the school division, for that amount. The school division's insurance company, Sweaty Hands Insurance Company, needed to defend itself against such a claim and therefore required the school division, the superintendent, the principal, the physical education department head, and Boris to provide all of the documentation about how the campfire and s'more escapade met the grade 12 physical education curricular outcomes in order to fight the claim by Good Hands Insurance Company. Suddenly, Boris the self-professed "engaged learning" master finds himself smothered not only in sticky marshmallow goop but also in voluminous amounts of paperwork he must submit to Sweaty Hands Insurance Company. Needless to say, all outdoor activities of the school division had to be suspended during this entire time-consuming process.

What the school trustees and the school officials need to be aware of is that insurance companies would prefer not to have to pay if they do not have to. If someone is found to be culpable, namely blameworthy by being reckless or negligent, the insurance company may not have to pay. Far too many school leaders live under the false illusion that they do not need to worry about calamities or perils because they are insured. What they need to know is that, if they apply some basic operational principles to the work of leading schools, they may avoid or lessen the likelihood of becoming a "subrogee," like Boris did.

- **Principle 4.6:** *Clearly identify the risk level associated with any given business operation, and ask people if they are willing to accept it.*
- **Practice 4.6:** *Risking other people's money, careers, and safety requires not only a moral compass but also the willingness to take "no" for an answer.*

THE ACCOUNTABILITY CHALLENGE

Accountability is often mentioned in a variety of contexts, but what does it really mean? Accountability may be described as being obliged to explain or justify one's actions and requires reporting both the actions and the results of those actions. The fundamentals of effective accountability require a subordinate to provide to his or her superior with an account of what has been done, the level of success achieved, and justifiable explanations to support results.

This process allows the recognition of achievement and timely corrective action, but it also requires a commitment from all individuals to undertake their responsibilities and to account to superiors for what they have done.

Explaining specific actions and providing information as to how the responsibility has been discharged allows those who have delegated this responsibility to assess whether responsibilities have been exercised as intended. This assessment may include a system for rewards and sanctions related to achievement, or lack of achievement, of results.

In the case of a superior/subordinate relationship, even though responsibility may have been delegated to a subordinate, the superior cannot relinquish his or her own accountability. Ultimate accountability remains with the superior, who must demonstrate adequate supervision of subordinates, as it is the superior who will ultimately be held responsible for subordinates' actions.

In addition, accountability also entails a requirement to commit to achieving responsible relationships that consider organizational values, ethics, and professional standards. Leaders are truly accountable if they

- say what they are going to do, how it will be accomplished, and to what extent it will be accomplished;
- believe in what they said they would do;
- are willing to stake their professional reputations on meeting, even if only partially so, their stated commitments and
- demonstrate explicitly what they have done during their tenure as a leader.

It is a fact that different employees have different relationships with the concept of accountability. Some arrive at the job with a well-developed sense of it, and others will need professional development, conversations, and prompting to learn accountability standards. A positive attitude toward accountability is often found in individuals with strong personal ethics and values. All staff need to have examples of leaders modeling these four phases of accountability. That said, an accountability framework impacts all levels within an organization and should not be seen as a function or practice of senior management only. A culture of accountability needs commitment from the highest levels of management to ensure that it is developed and nurtured and needs to be developed throughout every level of a school's personnel—accountability does not just happen.

It is worth reminding you how this chapter begins: Educating someone else's children involves risk. It would be reckless to suggest that all uncertainty can be or should be eliminated from the process of formal schooling. Students would become immune to learning if we tried to bubble wrap them and insulate them from learning.

What is required from educational leaders is a deliberate and careful assessment of the risks associated with schooling given the rewards that are derived from it. We need principals and vice principals who remain constantly aware that they are in fact raising someone else's child. It is a trite euphemism to suggest that we ought to treat someone else's child as if she or he was our own. We have no right to expose anyone else's child to the risk we might be willing to subject our own children to.

SUMMARY

This chapter may seem like it has had a lot of ideas tossed into it, but hopefully you see that it was created as such for good reason. First, we see that adults need to stay grounded in good, safe, and ethical risk management practices. Children are possibly the most vulnerable sector of society, and mass education—also referred to as schooling—exposes children and youth to numerous forms of risk. That should not prevent parents from trusting that school principals are working tirelessly to minimize the unnecessary exposure to risk or managing the school operations to lessen the effects of exposure. It is sad, but there are some self-declared educational leaders who are, metaphorically speaking, busy flying around at 30,000 feet, which to them equates to "leadership." These self-declared leadership visionaries are often quite clueless about the responsibility they have to manage risk, which means that their perception of risk is not necessarily sharp. High-flying leaders generally balk at people's concerns for such humdrum topics as cafeteria floor safety or perfectly handled employment interviews. They simply do not want to be burdened by having to ask the right or the difficult questions that come with managing a school's operations. To them, it is just too much tedious and tiresome work. It is not what they are interested in doing.

The high flyers are not necessarily bad people or blissfully ignorant fools. Maybe they did not want to rock the boat, especially if that means acknowledging that they were uninformed of some of the risks associated with a particularly popular program or service. Or they resist asking questions because it might be seen as questioning a professional colleague's expertise, and most colleagues do not want to be challenged, regardless of how much they say they do. These school leaders neglect the often difficult and uncomfortable role of a leader. Sometimes in order to shake up the status quo, however, you have to be willing to admit that you do not know everything and that you need to ask some tough questions. The leaders who do ask the hard questions discover soon enough that, if something seems too good to be true, it usually is.

Second, the best leaders consult with a mix of people—people with different perspectives, backgrounds, and knowledge—to predict, assess, and minimize overexposure to risk. They consult with others not only within their own immediate spheres of influence but also in other industries and sectors. By contrast, too many educational leaders only seek counsel from like-minded people, and this turns into the "echo chamber" in which the only voices that are heard sound just like the leader's voice. Consequently, they do not listen to people who bring different points of view to the discussion. Staff with a contrarian thought, new evidence, or a question that disputes the contentions of the "club" soon learn to "put up or shut up." As a result, there is no critical testing of ideas or assumptions and their potential consequences. By contrast, good leaders welcome different opinions and points of view. Because of this, they are aware of potential risks and have the ability to make more informed and inevitably wiser decisions.

Third, the most effective leaders are people of good character. They have integrity, courage, and compassion. They are careful, prudent, and aware of their limitations. As such, they are sensitive about the risks of harming their students, staff, and school community members by taking on too much risk. They do their very best to make sure that any decision they make or any action taken by their organization that involves a "risk" does not exceed a threshold for what might be tolerated. Overall, they exhibit an unrelenting determination to contribute to the good of the organization they serve, the people who follow them, and the communities in which they operate. Leadership, like all creative acts, flourishes in environments where individuals are able to take calculated risks and maybe the rare uncalculated one. It is an important proposition to file away: There can be tremendous advances made when we learn from our mistakes. Concomitantly, some decisions can result in organizational ruin. We need to know the difference before we act.

Conclusion

Parting Thoughts

You cannot cross the sea merely by standing and staring at the water.
—Rabindranath Tagore, born in 1861 in Kolkata, India, who was the first Asian poet to be awarded the Nobel Prize for Literature for his groundbreaking collection of poems *Gitanjali*

At this point I have hopefully convinced you that principals are required by the very nature of their work to both manage and lead their schools in what might be described as a fishbowl of public scrutiny from the endless list of so-called stakeholders in education. Such an obligation for transparency has resulted in the public's increasingly unrealistic expectations that principals are experts in all facets of school administration and that vice principals are experts-in-training. I do not want to add to the performance anxiety that comes from chasing such impossible expectations of perfection. That is not what I have intended to present in this book.

I firmly believe that school-based administrators need to be given the chance to learn about and to be offered opportunities for guided practice and to be mentored in both leadership and management. And they need to be allowed to take a few missteps and even make a few mistakes. Leadership is about learning and teaching. It's about sharing key insights, providing some of the "know-how," and giving opportunities to individuals to develop the knowledge and skills required to fulfill the obligations of being the principal. It's about sharing important ideas that may help smooth out the bumpy ride that comes with learning to lead.

LEADERSHIP is demonstrated through both the habit of mind and the action of taking a principled approach to

- develop a vision for change that leads to increased opportunities and improved outcomes for students based on shared and explicit values and
- mobilize, enable, and humanely support a school's staff to cultivate and follow through on the targeted initiatives for achieving the student and school outcomes that the staff prizes.

MANAGEMENT is about acquiring the knowledge and skills to

- move from an idea or a vision to leverage the resources required for operationally implementing the priorities that have been set and
- sustain the energy and practices required to achieve the illusive goals we set for the education system.

I have to admit that I am somewhat embarrassed by the fact that far too many educational leadership professionals, my colleagues, have declared that the days of preparing superintendents and principals to be managers of schools is a thing of the past. In my opinion, this is a shame. The all too common harbingers of the twenty-first-century principalship have characterized management as a dinosaur that once upon a time rampantly roamed principal preparation programs and devoured the souls of school administrators. In response, principals run away from all considerations that anything that resembles a management approach might support any kind of improvements to the teaching and learning dynamic in schools. Like Latin, they have accepted bloated hyperbole proclaiming that management is a dead subject. Leadership, they believe, is the panacea, the single elixir that can remedy anything that ails.

It is not hard to understand the reason for such rejection. For far too long the ideas of influentials like Henri Fayol, who proposed a theory of management that could solve all the woes of social organizations, dominated principal training programs. Studying overly mechanized approaches to managing organizational life had a lasting and limiting impact on the preparation of school administrators during the majority of the past century. And, arguably, perhaps, for far too long the writings of scholars like William H. Whyte, who wrote the 1956 bestseller *The Organization Man*, had too much of an influence on the minds of those who ran the school administrator preparation programs in such ways that they pushed principals to narrowly focus their time and energy only on the technical-rational aspects of school administration. I admit that a shift was needed to move away from the false security offered through the scientization of administrative life. *Homo bureaucratis* most certainly needed to be put on ice.

However, as the pendulum swung in the rabid pursuit of leadership, many self-appointed ministers of leadership simply abdicated the responsibility of teaching school administrators how to manage the school's operations effectively. It has occurred to me that maybe some of those same zealots of educational leadership did not understand the basic principles of management, or at least it is possible that they did not know how to enact the theories they preferred not to espouse.

It seems foolish to ignore that the new currency is to frame the principal as a school leader, and this branding certainly brings with it a cachet that sounds awfully attractive to those who consume the books and attend the executive workshops or strategic professional development seminars. There is a marketing machine at work pumping out tomes with titles like *Be the Change: Instructional Leadership 101*, *How to Become a Curriculum Leader in Seven Easy Steps*, *Unleash Your Inner Transformational Leader*, or *Rise to the Top as the Leader of Leaders*. These are just a few of the appellations that are used to frame the new work of the "principal." The opportunities abound in contemporary literature for school leaders to express themselves, no doubt promoting the very fact that they ought to self-actualize while realizing their potential and understanding their leadership style. These are attractive topics. But style will not carry the day when a lack of investment in learning about real-life solutions to problems in personnel management, finance, and risk catch up with the visionaries.

What I am proposing in the text is not an unorthodox approach, at least not when we look hard at what has been and is still required in the work of the principal. The ideas I am offering, when placed beside some of the current literature on leadership vision, the ones that diminish the managerial aspects of the job, may be seen as a throwback to antiquated times. I have been called much worse than an administrative romantic. In such a spirit, I offer this work if for no other reason than to serve as a reminder that the ways in which principals apply leadership principles and management practices will ultimately determine the success they find in their roles and, to a degree, the success that students and teachers find in the schools they administer.

Management should not be consigned to the privy of the palatial grounds of what is taught in leadership preparation programs because someone once suggested that managerial concepts have little to do with vision, mission, culture building, and instructional supervision. While these calls to recast the work to idealized notions may tug at the hearts and minds of principals, how you manage the people, money, and risk demonstrates your ability to lead in real time with real people's lives. I am proposing that what has been lost in the artificial separation of management from leadership and the diminution of the potential of good management practices to affect tremendously positive organizational outcomes is the fact that effective management complements effectual leadership. Many of the culture-building and culture-shaping aspects of the job of being a principal or vice principal are accomplished through a fusion of leadership and management.

I am a proponent of school leadership, make no mistake about that commitment. I believe that leaders can and do make a difference in the lives of those who choose to follow them. The approach to leadership I am proposing and advocating, however, is one that recognizes that it is vitally important for those responsible for the long-term health of schools and school divisions to manage the operational aspects in a manner that is as prized as the one they hold about leadership. Admittedly, what I am advancing is not an easy endeavor.

This approach calls on thoughtful individuals who are willing to work hard to provide a vision for the school community to ensure the organizational well-being of the school or division. I am advocating that we need folks in the administrative roles of schools who do not accept the defeatist attitude that it is impossible to embody both leadership and management. It is about refusing to accept that the dichotomy between "either/or" is an inevitable reality of having to choose between leading and managing school operations.

There are admittedly some hard truths in education, and one of them is that not everyone is cut out be a vice principal, principal, or even a superintendent. At some point, the public was sold the notion that anyone who wants to be a leader simply can be, without having to do any work to develop the knowledge, skills, and dispositions to be regarded as one by others. I bristle at such unwarranted claims because, while a great many are told they too can lead, few have told them that to lead people well requires a commitment to the disciplined focus to become highly effective at managing complex organizations like schools.

After more than twenty years of experience in the field of educational administration, of trying to both manage and lead well, I can attest to the fact that the ones who do it exceptionally well—and I am still working at getting better at it myself—are able to focus on the future and the possibility that education holds for student achievement while keeping the organization's wheels greased and its engine running. They manage the operational aspects and lead at the same time. These are the individuals who all children, teachers, and parents deserve to have leading and managing schools.

Leading while managing means that those in administrative roles in schools bind themselves to an ongoing process of being and remaining attentive to what the hopes and wishes of the school community are, thus ensuring the needs of today without overlooking the possibilities of tomorrow. Conjuring up lofty goals for schools—"blue-sky thinking" as it is sometimes called in the management literature—without having the ability to take care of the daily business that accompanies teaching and learning for hundreds and sometimes thousands of other people's children is a dereliction of duty. It takes knowledge, skill, and commitment to put in place the scaffolding necessary to allow students to achieve great things over a sustained period of time. To use a metaphor from at least 120 years ago, there is absolutely nothing wrong with having your head in the clouds while your feet remain on solid ground.

The Latin phrase *non satis scire* ("to know is not enough") aptly describes what is needed if we are going to make a positive difference in the lives of our students. We have learned quite a bit about how the human mind works since the ancient Greek philosophers developed the distinction between knowing and doing when they termed one as *Epistêmê*, which is usually translated as "knowledge," and the other as *Technê*, often translated as "craft" or "art." It takes work and focus to bridge the knowing and doing gap. It requires cultivating a deep awareness of self and of others and then a willingness to develop the knowledge and skills that connect people together using that awareness in tangible ways to improve students' opportunities to find success at schools and in the years after they complete formal education.

As much as we live in an era where we have become convinced that there are no "off the shelf" solutions, we also exist in a time when we are inundated with books that offer to give us the "six secrets," "seven habits," or "fifty nifty tricks" of successful leadership even though we recognize that schools are becoming more complex organizations. We are sold the solutions to anything that supposedly ails schools, and it is packaged for simple consumption. It is a safe bet that, when it comes to leading a school, there is rarely going to be a perfect alignment between what worked in the past, what seems to be working right now, and what might work in the future. Yes, what I am offering is a mighty challenge—leading and managing schools—one that is not only worth pursuing but also worth supporting.

When it comes to leading and managing schools, however, deciding how best to proceed is going to require a lot of both thinking and doing. It requires wisdom; not just any form of wisdom but rather a *particular* form of wisdom. What we need school leaders to know and do is best understood as that quality that Aristotle referred to as *Phronesis*—practical wisdom. It is a wisdom that involves deciding how best to proceed in a given situation while at the same time having the ability to reflect about whether the means chosen today will improve people's likelihood of living well in the future. It is a wisdom that looks at how today's decisions affect tomorrow's possibilities and honor the past. It means creating the organizational conditions under which today's students and staff can perform exceptionally well and flourish while offering hope that the next generation of students and staff will prosper at least as well, if not better.

Time for a minor confession: I work with some fine colleagues who think I spend far too much time telling educators "tales from the trenches" and who, in their wry attempts to sound witty, have labeled me an "educational pessimist." They would rather I be more upbeat and jovial with my message to school administrators. Over lukewarm coffee and terribly pasty muffins, they inform me that they would prefer I say: "Hey, anyone can do this hard leadership thing. It's not that hard. Just sign up for more courses, listen to the learned academics, and let us run your professional development workshops." They try to feign a smile to make me feel appreciated but really wish that I would simply get with the program, where the "program" is this positivistic sell that frames school leadership as a warm and cozy career choice. But I refuse to sell such snake oil. There is no cure-all remedy, and if one exists, I am most certain that we in academia do not possess it or know when to use it best.

I have also been labeled a bit of a "glib optimist" by others who think I am delusional in my belief that it is possible to help prepare individuals for the hard work to both lead and manage schools. At faculty events, with a cheap or free glass of wine in hand, they tell me that they remain unconvinced that there is a cadre of women and men who are capable of both leading and managing schools exceptionally well. "No one person can be expected to do both," they claim. Obviously, I disagree.

If I were given the opportunity, I think I would characterize myself as an optimistic realist. I believe the work that teachers, principals, and superintendents do is critically important in shaping the world we live in as it exists now and as it will exist in the future. And I think there are plenty of good people who are willing to take up the challenges associated with leading and managing school operations. What I am proposing is that we—those of us given the opportunity to shape the ideas and sharpen the skills of principals—ought to help prepare the folks who we ask to take on the hard work of thinking deliberatively, deciding wisely, and acting ethically in a concrete way. As I have previously stated, this is, in fact, the real test of those who suggest they are committed to developing the next generation of school leaders.

Leadership preparation is not about writing a lot of words bound in books with fancy titles and then asking administrators to read them, memorize a few key quotes, and regurgitate them in response to questions of their competency. Such offerings are a sham. I have witnessed scores of women and men who are willing to commit to the efforts to lead schools who would not mind the benefit of some concrete "how-to" managerial support as they learn to lead.

I therefore offer this book with the hope that it might offer some practical insight on synthesizing the "knowing" and "doing" of educational administration and of operating schools in particular. I believe that far too many individuals have bought into a highly marketed discourse that proposes that leadership without management can yield effective schools and school divisions. We all need both. Having principles that inform professional practice is as important today as it was over a century ago.

I have attempted to bridge the dichotomy that exists between being both leader and steward of one of society's most important social institutions:

schools. The book was written with the belief that it is possible to learn things and even enact them when you accept the responsibilities associated with being a principal or vice principal, but I have also tried to offer a ladder of sorts to scale the walls of leadership. Schools need leaders who are visionary thinkers and are equally capable of skillfully managing the business operations of the complex social organizations that schools are. Now that you are done reading, I hope you might agree with me that it is not only imperative to nurture such capabilities in people but also that it is possible for principals to perform both well.

Works Cited

Andrejeviv, Mark. 2013. *Infoglut: How Too Much Information Is Changing the Way We Think and Know*. New York: Routledge.

Blanchard, Ken, and Spencer Johnson. 2015. *The New One Minute Manager*. New York: HarperCollins.

Carroll, Lewis. 1993. *Alice in Wonderland*. New York: Drover.

Collins, Jim. 2001. *Good to Great: Why Some Companies Make the Leap and Others Don't*. New York: Harper Business.

Darling-Hammond, Linda. 2012. *Creating a Comprehensive System for Evaluating and Supporting Effective Teaching*. Stanford, CA: Stanford Center for Opportunity Policy in Education.

Darling-Hammond, Linda, and John Bransford. 2005. *Preparing Teachers for a Changing World: What Teachers Should Learn and Be Able to Do*. San Francisco, CA: Jossey-Bass.

Fullan, Michael. 2005. *Leadership and Sustainability: Systems Thinkers in Action*. Thousand Oaks, CA: Corwin.

Hayes James, Erika, and Lynn Perry Wooten. 2013. *Leading under Pressure: From Surviving to Thriving before, during, and after a Crisis*. New York: Routledge.

Peterson, Kenneth. *Effective Teacher Hiring: A Guide to Getting the Best*. Alexandria, VA: ASCD.

Smith, Robert, and Thomas D. Lynch. 2003. *Public Budgeting in America*. New York: Pearson.

Taleb, Nassim Nicholas. 2010. *The Black Swan: The Impact of the Highly Improbable*. Second edition. New York: Random House.

Index

About the Author

Jerome Cranston, PhD, is the executive director of student engagement and academic success and also an associate professor of educational administration at the University of Manitoba. Most recently, he has served in a university academic administrator position overseeing a staff of over one hundred people and a multimillion-dollar budget. Prior to that, he spent sixteen years in the K–12 education system as a teacher, principal, and superintendent in a career that spanned Canada's "prairie" provinces. He considers himself to be both a scholar and a practitioner in the broad field of educational administration, management, and leadership.

Dr. Cranston researches and teaches as part of a transdisciplinary international "community of inquiry" on topics of education, social injustice, peace, and human rights education. Dr. Cranston's work on teachers' conceptions of peace in postgenocide Rwanda earned him a 2015 American Educational Research Association Award for peace education. He is a sought-after workshop presenter by school divisions and teachers' and school leaders' professional associations on topics related to effectively leading and managing school teams and operations. He is fortunate to have married his best friend and contributed to the development of three amazing grown children.